Your Attention is Sacred Except on
Social Media

Your Attention is Sacred
Except on Social Media

Amelia Hruby

CONTENTS

Introduction

This tiny book you're holding in your hands — or reading on a screen — started off as a podcast called *Off the Grid*. That show began as a way of sharing my journey of leaving social media and starting a business without it. Then it evolved into conversations with creative small business owners and artists around the world.

At first, I thought the podcast was just about social media: how we got on these platforms, what they did to us, and the ways we could leave them behind. But over time, I realized that *Off the Grid* was about so much more than social media. It is, in fact, about *attention*: the things we pay attention to (or don't), the reasons we feel like we can't pay attention to anything anymore, and why we call it "paying" attention to begin with. I also realized that *Off the Grid* is more than just a podcast. So I decided to write this book.

In these pages, I'm going to unpack what "attention" means and why it seems to be the crisis of our times. I want to reconsider the concept of the "attention economy" and why I think conceiving of attention as an economic resource is misguided. I also want to explore why the pervasive adoption of social media has made attention *feel* so scarce — and remedies for how we can feel better online and offline. Along the way,

I'll talk about apps, algorithms, and addiction. I'll also explore creativity, community, and what makes attention sacred.

Before you begin reading, it's probably helpful to know that I left social media in 2021 and have not been active on any of the popular platforms since. While this book isn't anti-social media, it is definitely critical of social media. And my critiques are informed by my decade of being very active on social media (from 2009–2021), as well by the interviews I've done for *Off the Grid* and by my academic background. I have a PhD in philosophy, which certainly impacts how I see the world and how I put together an argument (hence why there are so many endnotes[1]).

This book is a philosophical, practical, and spiritual manifesto. At some moments, I lean into critical analysis, and at others I center on my personal experience. The chapters can be read together or separately, in order or not. If there's a section that intrigues you, head there first. If another bores you, skip ahead. If the first two chapters are too academic for your taste, go straight to the third, where everything gets spiritual and practical again. I've also included reflection questions at the end of each chapter, so you can integrate and implement these ideas in your life.

Here's my ultimate goal for this manifesto: **I want to explain how the two most prominent ways we talk about our experiences online — the attention economy and the algorithm — trap us in a specific experience of the internet and force us to become striving producers or passive consumers.** Then I want to offer another framework for cultivating our attention online *and* offline, that allows us to reclaim our agency and our place in the world in the process.

My hope for you, dear reader, is that you'll see some of your own experiences with social media reflected in these pages. I also hope that reading this might inspire you to journey down the path of reclaiming your attention, releasing all the reasons you "should" be on social media, and taking time to reinvest in other areas of your life.

As the title of this book asserts, *your attention is sacred*. I don't take that for granted as you lend it to me here. I promise to treat it with the honesty, reverence, and joy that I believe you and your attention deserve. *Let's dive in.*

Don't forget to take a deep breath as we begin.

1

Against the Attention Economy

We live in an era of attention. While wars rage, the planet heats, and our political systems become increasingly unstable, it seems that attention has somehow become our scarcest resource. Rarer than water, oil, or common sense, attention is what we never have enough of — at least if you listen to Americans on the internet.

I think the scarcity of attention seems like a ubiquitous fact, because we can feel the effects that constant phone use, notification overload, and the never-ending scroll of social media have on our bodies and our minds. We're tired. We're stressed. We're hunched over our screens. We can't put our devices down, even when they trigger our carpal tunnel. We have trouble paying attention to anything that isn't a 15-second video clip or doesn't move at 1.5x-speed.

While we may theoretically understand that gas prices are rising due to lower oil reserves, or that the weather is more extreme due to global warming — for those of us who live in the relative "safety" of US and European empire, the pressing concern we might *feel* each day is the conflict between how much we're asked to pay attention and how little attention we have to give. This tension is increasingly ever-present and shows up in our disrupted sleep, exhausted bodies, and dys-regulated nervous systems.

Because attention feels so scarce, many people have started referring to attention in economic terms. According to these people, attention is a scarce resource, and economics is how we distribute scarce resources. So we lament "the attention economy" in 140 characters or less as we scroll social media for "just one more minute" and quietly double-tap memes on our way to sleep each night.

Even though my tone is rather flippant, when I say "we" here, I very much consider myself in this group. When I was active on social media, I spent hours and hours on the apps each day. I scrolled for joy, validation, connection, even for doom. I used Instagram to express what I cared about per-sonally and to learn what I cared about politically. And in the four years I've been off social media, I still find myself reach-ing for the scroll to soothe, sate, or exacerbate my feelings. My attention can still feel fractured, scattered, or limited by how I spend time online — even though I now know that my atten-tion is a fluid, flexible, and creative faculty, rather than a lim-ited resource.

In this chapter, I want to sort through our understandings of "attention" and "economy" before returning to the con-cept of the "attention economy" to share why I think this phrase reflects and reinforces a fundamental misunderstand-ing of what attention is and how it functions.

We may live in a time saturated with demands for our attention, but that doesn't mean our attention is scarce. Once we realize that attention is a creative resource connected to our most human capabilities, we can reclaim our attention and redirect it in powerful ways.

But I'm getting ahead of myself. Let's begin by breaking down "attention," "economy," and the "attention economy." Please indulge me as we begin our journey etymologically.[2] We'll start with the word "attention."

ATTENTION

The word "attention" evolved from the French *attendere*, which means "to stretch toward." This comes from the prefix *ad* meaning "to, toward" and *tendere* meaning "stretch." *Tendere* itself comes from the Proto-Indo-European morpheme *ten* which is also the root of the words "tend" and "tender" — an association that I love.[3]

Fast-forwarding to the present day, attention is now broadly defined as applying the mind to something, noticing it, or directing your senses toward it.[4] The concept of attention has been theorized by the most prominent modern philosophers, from René Descartes to Immanuel Kant. It has also been present in psychology research since the field's scientific founding in the late nineteenth century. There, William James' early definition of attention is widely quoted as "the taking possession by the mind, in clear and vivid form, of one out of what seem several simultaneously possible objects or trains of thought."[5] Paraphrased, **attention is how our minds notice one thing among many.**

It would be impossible to summarize the centuries of philosophical and psychological research on attention here briefly, but as a philosopher of feminist aesthetics, I find myself particularly drawn to theories of attention from those fields. In my dissertation, I joined many readers of Kant who argue that his understanding of aesthetics involves the cultivation of a certain kind of attention that blends imagination and understanding.[6]

Kant's work also influenced Simone Weil's writings on attention, including her famous quotation: "Attention is the rarest and purest form of generosity."[7] Her work suggests that attention is something we *give* to others. This contrasts to the common phrasing "pay attention," which moves attention into transactional terms, losing generosity in the process.

As I write this, my favorite way to understand "attention" is to take apart the word itself as follows:

Attention — Attend to — Tend to

At its simplest, I believe attention is how we tend to the world. It's how we stretch toward people, places, things, and experiences with our mind, body, or spirit.

Attention is what's happening when we see something (or not), hear something (or not), and feel something (or fail to). It's the fundamental aperture of human consciousness and connection. We attend to the things we care about or the things we're required to care about, and the quality of our attention is inherent to the quality of our lives.

Attention is a vast and complicated topic, but it's also something we each do everyday. We look. We hear. We feel. We pay attention, or we give it. I think the ubiquity and daily quality of our attention is precisely what's at stake in the attention economy. As we journey there, we'll move to unpacking the history of the word "economy" next.

ECONOMY

The word "economy" originates from the Greek *oikonomos*, which meant household manager. Over time, this became *oeconomia* in Latin and *yconomie* in French, and the word "economy" emerged in English in the 1500s.

Looking at the origins of the word, *oikonomos* combines *oiko* and *nomos*. In ancient Greek, *oiko* referred to the household and the family. *Nomos* is often cited as meaning "law," but it has a more contested philosophical conception. In fact, the Sophists spent the fourth and fifth centuries debating the relationship between *nomos* and *phusis* or law and nature. This was basically the age-old might versus right argument, and it gives us a hint as to how power has been embedded in economics from the beginning.

Fast-forwarding to the present day, a quick Google search will tell you that the economy is "the wealth and resources of a country or region, especially in terms of the production and consumption of goods and services."[8] This conception of the economy gained popularity in the U.S. around the Great Depression, when poverty became apparent in everyday life. To combat low morale, U.S. government statistician Simon Kuznets introduced the concept of Gross Domestic Product (GDP) as a way of calculating productivity and signaling to the American public that conditions were improving, even if their households continued to struggle and poverty was evident around them.

So what is GDP? In short, it's a single metric that calculates the value of all goods and services produced in a country in a specific period. According to the U.S. Bureau of Economic Analysis, "The percentage that GDP grew (or shrank) from one period to another is an important way for Americans to gauge how their economy is doing."[9]

Essentially, when the economy is tied to the GDP, the strongest sign of a "good" economy is an increase in production. **Since the Great Depression, economic growth, material productivity, and national well-being have been inexorably intertwined.**

Alongside the rise of productivity as the primary measure of economic well-being, there's another concept that emerged in the first half of the twentieth century that has deeply impacted our understanding of the economy today. In 1932, British economist Lionel Robbins published "An Essay on the Nature and Significance of Economic Science," where he argued that economics is *the study of how humans negotiate their limited time with their expansive desires.*

Robbins' writings are often cited as the beginning of the "scarcity definition of economics." This tradition argues that economics is a study of how scarce resources are distributed. In fact, this is now how the American Economics Association defines economics, where it says economics is "the study of scarcity, the study of how people use resources and respond to incentives, or the study of decision-making."[10]

The scarcity definition of economics expanded our contemporary conception of the economy beyond both money and production and into the realm of decision-making. In doing so, it situated the complex negotiation between supply and demand at the heart of economics. Scarcity became the fundamental factor that motivates how we make decisions about spending our time or money *and* how we create and accumulate wealth, either as an individual or as a nation.

What does that mean for us? Well, if we look to the history of the word "economy," we can see how the Western conception of economics began with household management, developed the GDP to emphasize national productivity over household well-being, and then embedded scarcity at the heart of every economic transaction. As I've done this research, I've begun to trace a direct line between my household funds and my scarcity mindset. And honestly, it enrages me!

I don't agree with these economists' ideas that productivity and scarcity are at the heart of our households or societies. But I do feel the impact of their ideas in my life, every time I debate a purchase, put something on a credit card, or feel an overwhelming sense that there isn't enough to go around.

When Robbins asserted that economics was about negotiating our limited time with our expansive desires that brought every decision I make into the realm of economics. And if economics is embedded in all my decisions, then by its own definition, scarcity is there too. So how can I escape that?

For me, the answer emerges by uncovering the false scarcity at the heart of economics which is also at the heart of the attention economy. But before we get there — I've shared this brief overview of the history of the word "economy" and the concept of "economics," because I think it's important to see two things:

First, that neither productivity nor scarcity have *always* been a part of the "economy." Those values were embedded in our economy and culture to serve the powers that be.

And second, that **at this point, any time we use an economic model to make sense of something, scarcity and productivity are probably coming along with it**. Those values have been so deeply embedded in economics that the whole concept is now defined by them.

At the end of this book, I'll contrast the origins of the "economy" with those of "ecology" to explore other models for how we might understand attention. But for now, let's move to the "attention economy."

THE ATTENTION ECONOMY

Now that we've explored "attention" and "economy" as separate concepts, we can begin to unpack what they mean when they're combined. The phrase "attention economy" was initially coined by Herbert A. Simon in the late 1960s as a theory of how to handle information overload as more and more data became available with computers.

Throughout human history, the amount any one person or group of people could know had been limited by their context, community, and capability. Information beyond one's local or national communities had to be retrieved personally (through art or travel) or politically (through trade or war). As a result, having more information often meant having more power, and so knowledge was guarded rigorously.

But with the invention of computers — and the rapid rise of computing power from the 1990s to 2000s — more data was being collected, stored, and analyzed than ever before. Pretty quickly, there was more information than people could ever process, and all of this information was connected through the global web of the internet.

While information had previously been in short supply, it was no longer a scarce resource. Servers were swimming in oceans of data and algorithmic power. What became scarce instead was the human ability to sort through, make sense of, and attend to all this information. There simply wasn't enough time for any person to process it all in their limited lifespan. The supply and demand had flipped. **Information was no longer a rare economic resource. Now, our attention was.**[11]

Following up on this theory decades later, in 2001, Thomas H. Davenport and John C. Beck wrote the book *The Attention Economy* where they proposed that attention was the new currency that businesses needed to be accumulating and trading with. They cited the challenges of the modern workplace and argued that:

> "In this new economy, capital, labor, information, and knowledge are all in plentiful supply. It's easy to start a business, to get access to customers and markets, to develop a strategy, to put up a website, to design ads and commercials. What's in short supply is human attention. Telecommunications bandwidth is not a problem, but human bandwidth is." [12]

Like Simon before them, Davenport and Beck found that information was now abundant, while attention was scarce. Their book served as a step-by-step guide for companies seeking to capture, manage, and exploit their employees' and customers' attention. They explained common workplace problems like how employees who used to receive a few memos a week now received over 200 emails a day, and they offered organizational processes for managing that flow of information as managing individuals' attention.

Davenport and Beck uncovered how, even though work hours were limited, workers' labor could be maximized by fine-tuning the attention paid to tasks at hand. They also began to trace how these internal methods could be applied to external communications and marketing. It wasn't just about employees' attention but also about customers' attention. In essence, they converted the adage "time is money" into "attention is money" — and changed our lives in the process.

In researching this chapter, I found it fascinating that these theories of the attention economy have been around in nascent form for over 50 years and in full fruition for over 20 years. But while they may have once seemed like niche interests in business or economics, the global adoption of social media and the rise of influencer marketing has made the attention economy an overwhelming force in today's world.

This is how we get new guides like Gary Vaynerchuk's 2024 book *Day Trading Attention*, where marketers are taught how to locate areas of "underpriced" attention and sell to folks there. It's also why my claim at the opening of this chapter that attention is now considered "rarer than water, oil, or common sense" isn't intended as hyperbole. As I'm writing this, *New York Times* bestselling author Chris Hayes has just published a book where the subtitle is "How Attention Became the World's Most Endangered Resource." I don't agree with that claim, but it's certainly out there and not something I'm inventing or exaggerating.

To conclude our exploration of attention, economy, and the attention economy, I want to distill the reasoning of the "attention economy" down to a simple logic that begins with Robbins' understanding of economics as *limited time versus expansive desires* and eventually leads us to social media.

Here's the logic —

First —

As human beings, we are limited by our bodily capacities and our finite lifespans.

Attention is a cognitive experience, happening in our mind and our body.

As such, our attention is a limited resource and is inherently scarce.

Then —

Economics is the study of scarce resources and how they're distributed.

As such, economics is the correct framework to study attention, since it is a scarce resource.

Thus, the attention economy is the study of the scarcity of our attention and how it can be distributed.

I think this logic makes sense in an abstract way: *life is finite, so attention is finite, and we use an economic model to study finite resources.* But when we follow our attention down the economic rabbit hole, we can quickly see how this reasoning has paved the way for the accumulation and exploitation of attention by major corporations and tech companies. We'll explore this more in the next chapter on algorithms, but for now let me paint the picture of how this works in brief.

As attention has been pooled, measured, and monetized on social media platforms, the individual experience of attention has been scaled up into a globally accepted currency. Platforms and creators are inventing new methods for gathering and converting this currency every day. Just look at the exponential increase in ways to scroll, swipe, and double-tap. Or notice how even casual users of social media apps are inundated with metrics for likes, comments, and engagement. Then track the rise of ads, influencer marketing, livestreaming, and subscription models for turning our attention into cold hard cash.

We are currently living through the mass conversion of attention into money. Through the power of cleverness and Capitalism, attention has been fully commodified, and the attention economy has taken over... *voila!*

AGAINST THE ATTENTION ECONOMY

As a description of how attention has been commodified, I think that the attention economy makes a lot of sense. Attention gathered on social media platforms can be a proxy for financial or political power. We see this playing out in our local, national, and global communities right now as internet-famous celebrities become politicians and presidents.

My issue with the attention economy is less about how it describes the complexity of our current moment, and more about the premises that undergird it all. As I laid out in the last section, the attention economy requires — or, at least, takes for granted — that attention is a scarce resource; that's what makes it economic. And while I know that attention *feels* like a scarce resource for so many of us, I don't think it actually is.

The economic interpretation of attention is grounded in the idea that attention is limited by our bodily capacity and lifespan; human beings are finite and information is infinite. *There just isn't enough time to pay attention to everything*, they say. *Because there's too much information now*, they say. *And our lives are too short*, they say.

But I think that attention is (and always has been) more expansive than this simple equation allows. Paying attention to "everything" has never been possible, because the world has always been so much more than a single human life. **No one has ever been able to pay attention to all the information at hand, and there's no need to take for granted that we should want, need, or desire to.**

Here's where I think attention economists get it wrong —

Embedded in Simon's original formulation of the attention economy is the idea that attention can be measured and counted, just like the massive amounts of data he originally defined attention against.

But what is one unit of attention? Is it the glance at my phone during a meeting? Is it the moment I zone out between one task and the next? Is it the lingering gaze I share with my partner in bed? Or the three things I'm thinking about at once while I wait to pick my dog up from the vet?

Measuring attention attempts to turn a complex, nebulous process into a binary experience — either I'm paying attention to something or I'm not. But is that really the case? I'm often doing one thing and "keeping an eye" on another. Even as I write these words, I'm thinking of what to type *and* noticing that my dog is snoring at my feet. I'm giving my attention to two things at once. Three things, if I also begin to notice that my back is sore. Four things, if I sense the shift in light through the window as a cloud covers the sun outside. Five things, if I also start to reflect on how many things is too many for this list.

This simple observation of my writing experience shows me that attention isn't binary like an on/off switch, nor is it countable in the sense of how many things I'm noticing (or not) at any given moment. It also can't be measured in any sense of "how long" I pay attention to something.

Attention is a layered and dynamic experience. There have always been and will always be more things happening than I can pay attention to. This is the joy of human life. That my body can function without my needing to "pay attention" to it. That the planet will rotate without my noticing.

What's at stake in attention is not that human beings are finite, while information is infinite, but that our lives are finite and life is infinite. And that doesn't mean that anything is scarce.

Attention economists thrive by convincing us that attention is scarce when it's not. And they aren't the first to succeed at this tactic — in fact Frederick Taylor did it with time before them. That's why I like to say that attention economists are the Taylorists of the social media era. *Let me explain.*

Frederick Taylor was an American engineer and one of the first management consultants. His work focused on improving industrial efficiency by systematizing and standardizing labor productivity, often through meticulously measuring work times with stopwatches. His thinking is called "Taylorism" and has been widely critiqued by Marxists and labor organizers for how it led to punitive working conditions like timed bathroom breaks, invasive body movement tracking, and inhumane speed-based performance goals.[13]

Taylor turned the infinite nature of time into a meticulously measurable resource in order to commodify labor. Likewise, the attention economy turns the infinite nature of our life into a false binary of paying attention or not. **Where Taylor made time scarce by forcing it onto the factory's clock, attention economists make attention scarce by forcing it onto screens and apps.**

But we don't have to take the clock or the screen for granted — just like we don't have to take time or life for granted. Rather, I believe that our very notions of time and life are in fact shaped by what and how we "pay" attention. It's not that attention is limited by time, but that attention and time are intertwined, even co-created. Yes, our lifespan may be limited in days and years. But that doesn't mean our lives don't stretch beyond that limited perspective.

ATTENTION AND TIME

The time-shifting power of attention is something I've learned from my own life and my study of Pauline Oliveros and her work on Deep Listening and Quantum Listening. Oliveros differentiates between hearing, listening, and deep or quantum listening. She argues that hearing is involuntary, because we hear sound whether we want to or not. In contrast, listening actively directs our attention to what we've heard. As she puts it, *we hear in order to listen*. Listening is how we give our attention to what we hear.

I can attest from my experience as an audio editor and podcast producer that we can train ourselves to listen closer (or deeper), and when we do, we begin to hear more. After years of focusing my attention on sounds, I hear things I never would have before I did this work. Both my voluntary and involuntary attention have radically shifted and irrevocably changed. If we remember that the root of attention is *tendere* (to stretch), I am stretched open toward the world. My attentive capacity has been altered. I can take in more than before, and I feel less limited (in time and in attention) than ever.

This shift in the capacity of my attention is another clue that attention can't be measured in units or counted on a clock. To continue following Oliveros, she also explores how our attention can be radically altered *in time* by arguing that Deep Listening can become Quantum Listening. She writes:

"Quantum Listening is listening in all sense modes to or for the least possible differences in any component part of a form or process while perceiving the whole and sensing change. The Quantum Listener listens to listening. Quantum Listening simultaneously creates and changes what is perceived. The perceiver and the perceived co-create through the listening effect. All sounds are included in the field. This creates potential, cultivates surprises, opens the imagination and approaches and even plunges over the edges of perception into the mystery of the universe predicted by quantum field theory."[14]

Quantum Listening rejects binaries, units, and simple forms of measurement like clock-time. It is a practice of attention that directs us toward attention itself, or, as Oliveros puts it, toward "listening to our listening."

Learning about Quantum Listening finally helped me understand why time can be so slippery when I'm editing audio — because the quality of my attention there is unlike anywhere else. When I really open all my senses to what I'm hearing, I plunge over the edges of perception into mystery. **A minute of audio can take hours to hear, if I'm listening to myself listen.**[15]

Like Oliveros, we can turn to physics to reconceive the human experience of time as not so limited as we may believe it to be. Einstein's experiments in special relativity showed that time and space aren't simply fixed. Instead, the faster you move in space, the more slowly you progress through time. Separately, new experiments suggest that time may be a result of quantum entanglement, a theory that shows how two systems can be so interlinked that they impact each other even when they are widely separated by space. Or, as Oliveros parses it: that the perceiver and the perceived can be co-created in their entanglement.

I am not a scientist, and I'm not here to make arguments for classical versus quantum physics. Turning to science in this way just reminds me that time is not as static or limited as I was taught by the Taylorists to believe. And this affirms my own experiences of time, where I find that some moments feel endlessly long while others pass almost instantaneously.

My present moment is fluid and shifting, and it's also impacted by the past and the future — as I see it and as my society tells me about it. As John S. Mbiti says in his prominent text *African Religions and Philosophy*, "Time has to be experienced in order to make sense or to become real. A person experiences time partly in his own individual life, and partly through the society which goes back many generations before his own birth."[16]

Again, time has to be experienced, and our experience of time is shaped by our attention to the past, present, and future. Any bored child who's watched every second tick by on a clock can tell you that sometimes attending to time itself makes it go by slowly. But attending to the things we're interested in and giving them our full attention can make time fall away.

Who hasn't "lost track of time" or "stretched time" by being present in a moment? As Black Futurist Rasheeda Phillips reminds us in her book *Dismantling the Master's Clock*, "Experiences of temporality can diverge significantly — even in the course of identical events, where one might perceive its passage as either dilated or accelerated in comparison to another person experiencing the same event."[17]

If we don't take time for granted — or if we refuse to agree that it's simply a static thing, moving forward tick-by-tock on the clock — then our attention isn't inherently a limited resource. And that means we don't need an economic model to describe it.

In fact, using an economic model to describe attention may be causing many of our problems in the first place. As Maria Bowler writes in her book *Making Time*, "Your productivity lands you in a civil war with your own finitude. A producer is defined by this inner war with scarcity... The paradox is that your arguments with how limited your time and energy are keep you feeling bound by them."[18] Like Bowler, I think the contemporary emphasis on the attention economy is making us all *believe* that attention is scarce, when in fact that's only the case in a limited way within a certain (problematic) framework.

The "attention economy" was articulated and designed in order to commodify our attention and sell it on the market. This is why it's so important to critique the attention economy. **When we concede that attention is an economic resource, we concede that our attention is productive and also "for sale."** That makes it far more difficult to imagine our attention as anything else, to relate to it differently, or to perceive it as abundant rather than scarce.

In this chapter, I've attempted to trace the history of the words "attention" and "economy," as well as the origins of the concept of the "attention economy."

I've done this to help us see how the idea that attention is scarce has been invented and enforced by the people who want us to be productive for their profit. But if we step out of the role of producer, attention can return to its timeless nature, limited only by the power of our imagination.

So now, I ask you:

What if, instead of being scarce, your attention was actually a quantum resource — abundant and entangled?

What if, even though your life may be limited, your attention could stretch through space and time?

What if you refused to relate to attention in economic terms? Does the frequency of your social media use make your attention feel scarce?

What if you could reclaim your attention and reshape your experience of time, society, and life itself? What would that look or feel like?

I invite you to pause here and reflect on these questions. They are deep, meaningful, and may take you to unexpected places.

When you're ready to continue, please move to the next chapter on algorithms. There we'll explore the disconnect between the existing problems algorithms are programmed to solve and the newfound problems social media has created.

2

Breaking up with "the Algorithm"

If you spend any time on social media these days (circa 2025), you're likely to come across people lamenting "the algorithm." With vague, hand-waving references, they may claim that "the algorithm" is responsible for not sharing their posts, not showing them posts, not surfacing the right things, surfacing too many things, shadow-banning their content, overexposing their content, surveilling them on the apps, surveilling them off the apps, electing our most recent president, and anything else online or offline that seems to be somehow impacted by social media.

And these people are not wrong! Social media feeds are algorithmically determined. Algorithms do shape our experiences of these platforms. And those online experiences bleed into our offline lives, reshaping societal trends, values, and events in the process.

What's unclear, however, is how these algorithms work and what exactly they might be responsible for. Since social media algorithms are owned by private companies who make them completely opaque to users, "the algorithm" has become a big black box that we can project all of our frustrations with social media and society onto. It's the new Invisible Hand that we plead with, bow down to, and attempt to subvert — depending on how we're using social media on any given day.

In this chapter, I want to take a step back from our contemporary understanding of "the algorithm" to talk about what algorithms really are, how they function on social media, and steps that we might take to "break up with the algorithm," so to speak. In the process, we will consider how much choice we really have on social media apps and where to relocate our interdependent agency. *Let's get free.*

WHAT EVEN IS AN ALGORITHM?

Like many of you reading this, I am not a programmer, and until very recently I had no clue what an algorithm really was. If you had forced me to explain an algorithm to you, I probably would've said something like "some code that makes decisions about what to show me?" And I wouldn't have been completely wrong! But I also wouldn't have been all that right, either.

To learn more about algorithms, I turned to the MIT Press Essential Knowledge Series, where Panos Louridas has helpfully written a book called *Algorithms* that introduced me to the subject and forms the basis of what I'll share here.

At their essence, algorithms are simply step-by-step ways to solve a problem. They existed long before computers did, and their methods of sequencing and patterning can be seen in ancient equations and musical rhythms.

The reason we program computers to run algorithms is simply because computers work really fast, so they can run complex algorithms pulling from huge datasets in a fraction of the time it would take people to do so. Here's how a typical algorithm works (again very simply):

We start with a problem.

We gather data related to that problem and feed that data into the algorithm.

The algorithm performs a series of choreographed steps to process the data — which may include sequencing, selecting, or iterating in a simple or very complex combination.

Through that process, the algorithm transforms the data into a solution to our problem.

When I was learning about algorithms, mapping was one of the first examples that helped me make sense of it all, so let's consider map apps like Apple Maps, Google Maps, or Waze, for instance.

We start with a problem: how do I get from Place A to Place B? Now, I could gather a ton of maps and sort through them myself, using a series of steps and priorities to choose the best path from one location to the next, or I could find an algorithm to do that for me.

Popular map apps have a data set of all road maps in the world, as well as information on construction, traffic, weather, and other things that impact travel. They also have an algorithm that's been designed to consider all this data and map a way for me to get from Place A to Place B on legal road-ways in the shortest amount of time.

The map apps' algorithm will always do this when I input two locations and request directions. But the app also in-cludes many options where I can make real-time adjustments to the algorithm and choose what it prioritizes as it constructs my path. For example, I can request that it prioritize public transit over driving, that it skip highways or toll roads, or that it find bike routes or walking paths.

I think map apps are a great example for wrapping our minds around an algorithm because they work on a clear problem with a clear dataset, and they find a clear solution. There is in fact one fastest way to get from Place A to Place B. The map app's algorithm can find that for me, and it can do it much faster — and with more up-to-date information — than I could!

That's why I'm glad that mapping apps exist. It used to take me forever to figure out the fastest route from one place to another, and often traffic would foil my best-made plans. Now I can use an app to make these decisions instantly, free-ing up my mental capacity and decision-making in the process.

While algorithms have grown increasingly complex with the rise of social media and generative AI, at their core, algo-rithms are simply tools for solving problems. They're not inherently good, bad, or evil (although they can certainly inherit the intentions and biases of their programmers). And in the case of map apps, I feel like an algorithm actually helped me get free! Or it at least helped me solve a problem I was *actually* having, so that I could then give my attention to other things.

Now let's turn to social media and see where algorithms go awry...

THE PROBLEM WITH SOCIAL MEDIA ALGORITHMS

As I just argued, algorithms in and of themselves are ways to solve a problem. Some algorithms solve our problems and that's that! But other algorithms... are much murkier in their intention and impact. Let's consider the evolution of two different social media apps to explore how and why this is the case. We'll begin with Facebook.

Facebook was founded by Mark Zuckerberg in 2004. At the time he was a student at Harvard, and the original "problem" the platform solved was social networking. In its initial incarnation, Facebook allowed Harvard students (then Ivy League students and university students writ large) to connect with their peers and share social updates. It helped users build and maintain a network of relationships, and at that time, the "data input" of the site was the users' contacts and social connections.

The platform functionality was creating profiles and posts (and pokes), but the early Facebook algorithm (at least in my memory of using it) offered up friend suggestions of people you might know based on who you were connected with. The problem was: we all needed, wanted, or had more friends than our mental capacity or a clunky Rolodex could keep track of. The Facebook algorithm sequenced and sorted connections to suggest people we might know or be interested in knowing. And, as a result, we were better able to start and maintain connections across social networks.

Here we can see that the problem, the data, and the solution are all aligned. I think this is why Facebook became so popular initially, and why so many of us actually made friends there. Now let's turn to a different sort of app: Pinterest.

Pinterest was founded in 2011 as a platform for collecting and pinning visual inspiration. It initially grew out of the founders noticing that users of their failed virtual catalog app, Tote, were saving and sharing items they liked but not purchasing them. So Pinterest was created for more of that saving and sharing, and users quickly brought their own problems to the app for its algorithm to solve.

For example, perhaps my problem is that I want to refresh my fall wardrobe, but I need inspiration. On Pinterest, I can search for fall fashion and pin my favorite images to my "fall wardrobe" board. Those images — along with my behavior of selecting them — is my data input. The Pinterest algorithm then uses that data from me as well as the behavior of other users to suggest similar images I might like. And of course, those images are hyperlinked to the actual items that I can purchase from brands or retailers. So I can find inspiration, receive recommendations, and purchase my fall wardrobe in one convenient place.

This is just one of many problems I might use Pinterest to solve. But in this instance, we can see how the problem, the data, and the solution are again aligned.[19]

These two examples show how **early social media algorithms were built to solve real problems for real people**, and the data they gathered from those people was appropriate to those problems.

What's happened over the past decade, however, is that social media apps are no longer clear about the problems they solve or the data they collect, and users are perhaps even less clear about what we hope these apps might help us with. In addition to that, the algorithms on these apps have become adaptive and changed in ways that we didn't anticipate. It's been a complicated journey since the early days of Facebook. *Let's break down that process.*

As social media apps grew, we saw them radically transform. Originally, these platforms had to effectively solve our problems in order to get us to use them. Facebook, Pinterest, and others had to prove their utility to people around the world. But as millions (then billions) of users flocked to these platforms, they became massively popular virtual spaces where we "had to be" in order to know what was happening in the world.

Because most social media platforms were free to use, they benefitted massively from the network effect. The more people that were on social media, the more value people found there, and the less they expected a platform to "do something" for them.

So social media platforms went from solving users' problems to being general spaces for information, entertainment, and connection. We saw companies like Facebook do things like launch games inside the platform, create television shows and streaming programs, and pivot to the metaverse and virtual reality technologies.

On the one hand, this is fine. More users, more value, and more use-cases aren't necessarily a bad thing. But the issue became twofold.

First, social media platforms are run by privately owned or publicly traded companies who need to make money. In the case of those with venture capital backing (which is basically all of them), they need to maximize profits and show returns for their investors. Getting people onto the platform by solving their problem(s) for free wasn't profitable. In fact, it was incredibly expensive to host users' data and run the algorithms that process it. **So once social media apps had gathered enough people on their platforms, the new "problem" their owners needed to solve was how to make money from the users they'd gathered there.**

That leads to our second issue: algorithms are built to solve problems, and now instead of prioritizing the problems that users were bringing to social media, the owners of these platforms prioritized getting the algorithms to solve their own problems around making money. The one-word solution to this problem was *ads*, and the many-word solution was: ads that are expertly, algorithmically targeted toward each user's unique interests as documented on these apps.

One of the watershed moments where we saw this happen was when Instagram removed their chronological feed in 2016. It used to be that, when you logged on to the app, you'd see the posts of everyone you followed in chronological order, with the most recent posts appearing first. This meant that you could scroll to the "end" of your feed, where you had caught up with everything new that had been posted since you last logged on. When the feed shifted from chronological to algorithmic, there was no more "end" of the feed. New posts were always suggested, now with recommendations of people you might want to follow or sponsored posts and ads from brands who'd paid to be featured in more feeds.

In the early days of this shift, I think many people actually appreciated the new algorithm. It helped them discover creators they really loved, and something I hear from many guests on my podcast is that they made a ton of friends on Instagram from 2014 to 2018.

But over the years, the sentiment about the Instagram algorithm has shifted dramatically. Users have gone from loving the app to hating "the algorithm" for all the reasons I mentioned at the start of this chapter: it's not sharing their posts, not showing them posts, not surfacing the right things, surfacing too many things, shadow-banning their content, and surveilling them on and the off the app.

It's all very opaque to users, because as Safiya Umoja Noble points out in her groundbreaking book *Algorithms of Oppression*, we never know when, why, or how these things are happening, because "it is impossible to know when and what influences proprietary algorithmic design, other than that human beings are designing them, and that they are not up for public discussion, except as we engage in critique and protest."[20]

The 2020 documentary *The Social Dilemma* was one of the first places that I saw people who'd been involved in the creation of major apps pull back the curtain on how social media algorithms functioned. The documentary argues that social media algorithms have been programmed to keep users on the app and engaging with the content there.

While this may seem like a neutral goal, the way that the algorithm has developed to solve this problem is incredibly problematic. When I spoke to Vickie Curtis — one of the writers of this documentary — for my podcast, she shared:

> "Google, Facebook, Twitter, Snapchat and TikTok [are] very secretive about what they're doing. So, it was really amazing to have access to people who had been on the inside and could sort of reveal the business model that is being adopted. Not only the effects it's having on the users, but also the effects that it's having on society at large. We really wanted the film to be able to look at not just the personal level of 'yeah, maybe you spend too much time on Instagram or you wasted half an hour on TikTok,' but to look at the effect on democracy, the effect on truth, the effect on our ability to communicate with one another and understand what's really going on versus what is a lie. All of a sud-

den that has these huge ripple effect consequences, and it becomes an existential crisis."[21]

What *The Social Dilemma* uncovered is that while social media algorithms may have been designed with the "neutral" goal of keeping users engaging on their platforms, those algorithms "discovered" that content that outrages users, pushes them to extremes, or plays to their unconscious biases is the most likely content to keep them on the apps. So the algorithms started serving users more of those kinds of content, and that shift had detrimental political effects. To name just two examples: the Cambridge Analytica scandal that helped elect Trump in 2016, and how the Facebook algorithm boosted the genocidal violence of the Myanmar military against the Rohingya people in 2017.

Curtis helped me see that individuals' actions were being influenced by social media algorithms on almost every level — whether we're consciously aware of it or not. In his book *Ten Arguments for Deleting Your Social Media Accounts Right Now*, computer scientist, technologist, and writer Jaron Lanier (who was featured in *The Social Dilemma*) explains how this algorithmic manipulation actually works:

> "Algorithms gorge on data about you, every second...
> [They] correlate what you do with what almost every-
> one else has done. The algorithms don't really under-
> stand you, but there is power in numbers, especially
> in large numbers. If a lot of other people who like the
> foods you like were also more easily put off by pictures

of a candidate portrayed in a pink border instead of a blue one, then you probably will be too, and no one needs to know why... Now everyone who is on social media is getting individualized, continuously adjusted stimuli, without a break, so long as they use their smartphones. What might once have been called advertising must now be understood as continuous behavior modification on a titanic scale."[22]

As Lanier points out, even though our social media feeds feel personal, that's only because social algorithms use collective data to do behavioral modification work at an individual level.

So "your algorithm" feels tailored to you specifically, even if it is actually just constructing a prediction of your behavior from a giant data set. This is why we all have such different social media feeds and varied triggers that the algorithm has learned will keep us engaged. You may be sucked into online arguments, so the app feeds you drama. Or you may only stay engaged with cute animal videos, so it feeds you more cats, dogs, cows, and goats.

At the end of the day, the goal of the social media platform owners — and thus the goal of their algorithm — is to keep you on the app, so you keep seeing ads and make a purchase that they can take a cut of. *And it's working*.

Capital One reported in late 2024 that over 1.4 billion (70%) of active users shop on Instagram, and 83% of users search for new brands and products on Instagram. They also reported that TikTok users spend $7 million *per day* shopping on TikTok, and that's only increased since.[23]

So what do we do with all of this? Well, what I hoped to help you see in this section is that **while social media algorithms used to solve our problems, those algorithms now power massive economic engines channeling billions in profits to venture-backed companies and their shareholders.**

While some algorithms may be neutral or even good, today's social media algorithms are of a different kind. They generate outrage, impact politics, and fuel consumerism. And, in the process, they make a lot of us feel bad. Plenty of research and reporting has been done to show that social media use increases rates of anxiety, depression, and irritability.[24] At this point, I don't know anyone who uses social media who doesn't find some aspect of their experience on the apps negative or problematic.

If you're reading this book, I'm assuming you're curious about changing your relationship to social media in some way — perhaps stepping back from the apps or away from social media altogether. *I think that's great!* And that you have options. So now let's talk about breaking up with an algorithm and what that might entail.

HOW TO BREAK UP WITH AN ALGORITHM

As we move toward practices and things you can do to shift your relationship to social media, I want to offer two levels of praxis: getting out of *your* algorithm and getting out of *the* algorithm.

I first heard the phrase "getting out of your algorithm" from Kate Smalley, who was a guest on my podcast in fall 2024.[25] In our conversation, we discussed what it feels like to be stuck in a loop of similarity when an algorithm serves you more and more limited options. This often results in feeling like you're in a "bubble," an "echo chamber," or a hall of mirrors where you only see endless iterations of one thing looking back at you as you scroll.

By "getting out of *your* algorithm," we're talking about popping that "bubble," inviting in new possibilities, and cultivating your own sense of taste — even on the apps. This level is great for folks who want to stay on social media but feel more intentional and sovereign in their experiences there.

The second level is what I think of as "getting out of *the* algorithm." This is a deeper level of critique, recognizing that social media impacts our offline experiences in profound ways and that we may need to exit the platforms altogether to truly reclaim our agency and attention. It's also the recognition that insofar as social media does shape offline experiences and aesthetics, we may never escape "the algorithm" entirely, but that doesn't mean we're beholden to it completely, either.

I'm not here to tell you that you have to leave social media, or even that you should. But I do want to offer some thoughts on why it's been necessary for me (and many others) to quit using social media apps. I also want to illustrate how you might come to that decision in your own way and on your own timeline. *Let's begin with getting out of your algorithm.*

GETTING OUT OF YOUR ALGORITHM

Before you can get out of your algorithm, it's important to recognize what it looks and feels like to be stuck in your algorithm. I described this before as a "loop of similarity" that I believe happens with algorithms that recommend things or serve us content based on our behavior.

Every time we watch or like something on a social media app, that behavior indicates to the algorithm that we might like something else similar to that thing. Over time the algorithm uses our behavior and the behavior of other people like us to more consistently predict what we'll like, what we'll love, and what we absolutely do not want to see.

At first, this can be exciting. You feel like you're developing your own sense of taste by honing in on exactly what you're into. But at a certain point, the algorithm "knows" what you want to see, and it serves you more and more and more of that. This is how Pinterest ends up showing me dozens of claw clips and twenty red sweaters in one scroll. It's also how YouTube knows I like watching mid-thirties women talk about romantasy books they've read recently, and now that's all I see in my feed. Over time, what once felt like we were figuring out "exactly what we like" can turn into feeling like we're only seeing one thing — or only seeing hundreds of iterations of one thing and nothing else.

In Jenny Odell's book *How to Do Nothing*, she describes how the Spotify algorithm has gotten her "stuck" in a loop of similarity with music. She writes:

"Over the years, the Spotify algorithms have correctly identified that I tend to like 'chill' music of a certain BPM ... As I continue to listen to the [Spotify-created] playlist, dutifully saving the songs that I like, the weekly playlist begins to hone in, if not on an archetypal song, then an archetypal mix — we could call this "the Jenny mix" — and other potential mixes are measured for their likeness to whatever the current archetype is."[26]

The "Jenny mix" is an example of what it feels like when the algorithm correctly constructs a predictive model of your behavior from a giant data set. The more Odell listens to her mix and saves songs she likes, the more similar songs Spotify recommends for her. And again, this can be satisfying, but it's also limited. As Odell explains, all other mixes are measured for how similar they are to "the Jenny mix," which means that recommended music will always be more and more similar to what she's already liked.

But so much of what makes life beautiful, unique, and full of joy is how it surprises and delights us — not simply how it delivers exactly what we expect. Over time, we can come to feel stuck in our loop of similarity rather than at home there. That's when I think we might want to "get out of our algorithm."

Odell offers an idea of how to begin this process when she explains her turn from listening to music on Spotify to listening to music on the radio. She says:

"I listen to the radio... Especially when I'm driving home late on Interstate 880, feeling anonymous in the dark, flat expanse, I'm comforted by the fact that some other people are hearing the same thing I am... More importantly, none of these stations ever play anything like 'the Jenny mix.' Instead they will occasionally play a song that I like even more than my archetypal song, in a different way and for reasons I can't really pinpoint... Especially with something as intuitively appealing or unappealing as music, to acknowledge that there's something I didn't know I liked is to be surprised not only by the song but by myself."[27]

I want to point out a few different aspects of this experience that help Odell break out of "the Jenny mix" or even "the Jenny algorithm." Foremost, there's the turn from app to radio, which moves from algorithm-curated to human-curated music experience. Then, there's the communal nature of listening with others. Radio happens in synchronous time. You tune in at that moment or you don't. So there's a sense of presence and giving your attention to it that can't be replicated by scrolling a social media or music feed. And finally, there's the delight of hearing and loving an unexpected song. As Odell shared, the experience of loving something she didn't expect allowed her to be surprised by the song *and* herself.

Getting to know ourselves isn't simply a matter of honing in on the One Singular Thing we love. Identity, preference and taste are multifaceted, relational and all exist in time. We need inputs that break the loop of similarity that the algorithm creates in order to access those aspects of ourselves. **That's the first step of getting out of your algorithm: finding new, unexpected inputs.**

If we follow Odell's example, it may seem like moving our lives offline could solve all our problems. But unfortunately, while algorithms largely function online, they also shape and impact our offline experiences. This is a phenomenon that Kyle Chayka explored in his 2024 book *Filterworld: How Algorithms Make Everything the Same*. There he describes the archetypal/algorithmic coffee shop. No matter where you go in the world, he proposes, you can find a coffee shop with white walls, reclaimed wood, Edison bulbs, and a letterboard menu on the wall. This is a result of our taste being shaped online by algorithms that eventually end up dictating the style and design of offline spaces. Getting out of your algorithm, then, requires popping the bubble of that filterworld. *So how do we do that?*

First another tactic that I don't think works: Sometimes people attempt to get out of their algorithm by modulating and chaoticizing their behavior on social media. They'll like unexpected things, seek out novelty, and try to shift what they see or engage with, hoping the algorithm will "take the hint" and start serving up different things.

In my experience, however, this strategy has a limited impact. The dataset is huge, relative to the limited amount we are seeing or doing, so the effect of a few tweaks is minimal. Additionally, what we see on social media also seems to be impacted by the people we are connected to. If they're not changing their behavior, that in turn limits our ability to influence the algorithm ourselves.

There's also a way that social media algorithms are actually already designed to randomize content and take this "chaotic" type of approach into account. Lanier explains, "Social media algorithms are usually 'adaptive,' which means they constantly make small changes to themselves in order to try to get better results... A little randomness is always present in this type of algorithm... Every once in a while an algorithm finds better settings by being jarred out of merely okay settings."[28]

Lanier even takes this analysis one step further to explain how this randomness can also lead to the dopamine bursts that fuel an addiction to social media. He says:

"When an algorithm is feeding experiences to a person, it turns out that the randomness that lubricates algorithmic adaptation can also feed human addiction. The algorithm is trying to capture the perfect parameters for manipulating a brain, while the brain, in order to seek out deeper meaning, is changing in response to the algorithm's experiments... Because the stimuli from the algorithm don't mean anything, because they genuinely are random, the brain isn't adapting to anything real, but to a fiction. That process—of becoming hooked on an elusive mirage—is addiction. As the algorithm tries to escape a rut, the human mind becomes stuck in one."[29]

Based on Lanier's insight, it seems very unlikely that we can beat the algorithm at its own game of randomness. In fact, injecting random content into the loop of similarity may only result in feeling (or being) more addicted to social media.

So what can we do to get out of our algorithm? Well, I think we can begin by following Odell's lead and seeking out experiences off the apps, with other people, that happen in synchronous time. It's perhaps a "boring" solution, but it's a meaningful one.

The antidote to being stuck in your algorithm is going elsewhere. You can do this online by going to platforms that are less algorithmically determined or whose algorithms don't prioritize profit and engagement. (I'm thinking here of going from Pinterest to an app like Are.na. — where both apps share visual blocks sorted onto boards, but only Pinterest prioritizes advertising and data tracking.) Or you can move offline and explore different spaces, relationships, and opportunities.

Even as we see algorithmic preference shaping our offline world, we can still find texture, difference, and surprise in our day-to-day lives. In some instances, it's about turning to what worked in the past — like listening to the radio or visiting a record store to find music recommendations. In other cases, we are invited to invent new things — like launching an online radio station or starting a music club that meets locally once a month to swap our favorite albums. And sometimes we might need to try things we expect we'll dislike, just to see if we surprise ourselves by actually enjoying them — like how I discovered heavy metal can be a perfect mood music for me in dark times.

When we feel stuck in our algorithm, it's because we've handed our attention and our agency over to an app to tell us what we like and what we should do. We've outsourced the cultivation of taste (in the case of recommendation algorithms) and connection (in the case of networking algorithms).

Turning toward less-extractive algorithms or offline spaces is one way to get out of our personal algorithm, but I think the true work we're called to do is to get out of "the algorithm" on a deeper level. We'll explore that next.

GETTING OUT OF "THE ALGORITHM"

In Panos Louridas' book *Algorithms*, he explains how algorithms are one way to solve a problem based on a dataset. Then he offers this warning:

> "When we try to find an algorithm to solve our problem, we should check that our problem meets the requirements of the algorithm. Otherwise the algorithm will not work; but note that an algorithm cannot tell us that it doesn't work... It will produce an answer that will be nonsense. It is up to us to make sure we are using the right tool for the right job."[30]

This warning was ringing in my ears as I worked on this chapter, because it helped me understand my intuition that *social media isn't the right tool for the job.*

While we've already gone through many of the harmful, real-world impacts that social media algorithms have had, I think there's still one major problem to elucidate: **We've started turning to "the algorithm" to solve problems it was never meant to solve.**

In fact, I think we turn to "the algorithm" to solve almost *any* problem we want to solve. And at times, we turn to "the algorithm" to tell us what problems we have.

This results in what programmers call "garbage in, garbage out." Whether we're searching for a red sweater, trying to reconnect with our college roommates, or sharing something vulnerable to meet others who've experienced it too, we go to social media apps and feed "the algorithm" all of our problems. Then we just scroll to see what it gives us back to us.

And it's not that our problems are garbage! I want you to find the right red sweater and your college roommate's new number and those people who get what you're going through! But we're taking all of that to a massively unwieldy dataset and asking an algorithm that was designed to do something totally different to solve these problems for us. And as Louridas explains, the algorithm can't tell us that we're inputting the wrong problem. So it just keeps doing its thing and churning out an "answer," but that "answer" is garbage.

With all of this in mind, I think that "getting out of the algorithm" first requires becoming more aware of your problems and how well they align with the algorithms of the apps where you go to solve them.

Need to get from Point A to Point B quickly? The map apps have you covered. Need to find the right red sweater? Maybe Pinterest can help with that. Need to track down your college roommate a decade later? Facebook is on it.

I think there are appropriate uses of these tools, and if we're using them to solve the problems they actually solve, then we may effectively be able to stay on social media and "get out of our algorithm"— if not out of *the* algorithm.

Here's the deeper issue: **social media algorithms have become so complex and their platform interfaces have become so determinate that, if we go to any of these apps to solve our problems, they're only going to offer solutions that fit within a very narrow box of what's possible.** And if we spend much time on these apps at all, they're going to dictate the problems we think we have and create new problems for us that aren't problems at all.

As we've traced here, social media algorithms have evolved to keep users on the apps and drive them toward purchases. They've created a very narrow set of behaviors possible on the apps (*like, comment, subscribe, buy*). In a certain sense, they've become consummate advertisers, constantly inventing and presenting problems to sell the products that will solve them.

Most of us just have to look at the receipts in our email inboxes as proof of this. To illustrate my point, here's a brief list of things social media influenced me to purchase that solved a problem I didn't have before I saw them:

An ice roller (I think for my face?)
An e-reader remote (so I can click differently?)
At least six pairs of leggings (for workouts I've never done)
A suitcase (that broke within six months)
An air fryer (...of course)
So. Many. Candles.
So. Much. Underwear.
Every skincare product I've ever owned

These purchases cost different amounts of money and had different degrees of impact on my life, but the thing that ties them together is that I bought them on impulse because I saw them on social media. I did that, because I was told I had a problem that needed solving, and I agreed — even if I had never noticed that problem before I saw the product. Looking back at my list, here are the problems those items told me I had.

Wrinkles
Lifting my arm
Being ugly (at the gym)
Being ugly (at the airport)
Not having enough time to use the oven
Not having enough time to make my house smell better
Being ugly under my clothes
Wrinkles

This list is a bit tongue-in-cheek, I can admit. But when I went back through my inbox to look at what I'd purchased and ask myself why I bought these things, most of the answers were in one of two camps: either I was told (typically subliminally) that something was "ugly," or I was told a product would save me time. When I lay it out this way, I can see so clearly how my purchasing tracks directly onto my deepest fears. I have been conditioned to believe that being "unattractive" is the ultimate sin for a woman. So I spend money to avoid that. And I feel like the world always wants more of my time that I can't get back. So I spend money to try to "save time" so I can "spend" it on different things.

Here we can see so much of what I wrote about the attention economy coming into play in my own life. And while I'd say that appealing to someone's fear to sell them something is more of an issue with advertising itself than it is with social media, we just have to go back to Lanier's argument I cited earlier to see how advertising and social media have collapsed into each other at this point.

When we're active on social media, we're consenting to hyper-personalized, constantly optimized advertising every moment we're online. As Lanier puts it, "What might once have been called advertising must now be understood as continuous behavior modification on a titanic scale."[31]

And we've not only consented to this, but embraced and celebrated it. Safiya Umoja Noble makes this argument about Google in *Algorithms of Oppression* where she says:

> "Google's monopoly status, coupled with its algorithm practices of biasing information toward the interests of the neoliberal capital and social elites in the United States, has resulted in a provision of information that purports to be credible but is actually a reflection of advertising interests. Stated another way, it can be argued that Google functions in the interests of its most influential paid advertisers or through an intersection of popular and commercial interests. Yet Google's users think of it as a public resource, generally free from commercial interest."[32]

We believe, trust, or hope that the algorithms on social media and search engines are solving our problems, but in fact our use of these platforms is just making money for the companies that own them.

This is where we get the saying "if something is free, you are the product." And it's why Noble argues that "Google benefits directly and materially from what can be called the 'labortainment' of users, when users consent to freely give away their labor and personal data for the use of Google and its products, resulting in incredible profit for the company."[33]

The same is true of social media users when we scroll and see ads, or, especially, when we make purchases through social app portals. Our data is constantly being extracted, and our attention is often being manipulated. We are laboring "freely" and making billions for tech companies in the process.

I worry that laying all of this out in this way makes it feel like "the algorithm" is inevitable, like it's a force we cannot escape, or like it is a compromise we must make to get our problems solved. I don't believe that's the case. **We are not inevitable victims of an extractive algorithmic world.**

That said, I think the first step of getting out of "the algorithm" is getting really clear about what problems it's solving for us. Because I think that there are very real problems that social media does solve. And depending on your social location, it may even be a lifesaver for you. *Let's acknowledge that!*

But after we make this list of how social media helps us, we also need to make a list of how social media harms us — and we need to meaningfully grapple with that harm.

Here are a few questions for you to begin that process:

What needs of yours are being met on social media?

How does any given app improve your life?

What problems does social media convince you that you have?

How does social media negatively impact your life, your work, or your mental health?

And then, stepping outside of your individual experience, *what impact do you see social media having on your local community, your national community, and the planet?*

In this section, I've tried to lay out my argument for how algorithms can solve our problems and, also, how social media algorithms negatively impact our lives — individually and collectively.

At the end of all this, I'm not here to convince you to leave social media. Instead, I'm asking you to ask yourself these questions, to make a pros and cons list, and then to weigh your lists against each other. Your inner compass has to guide you forward.

But in the spirit of this manifesto, let me be clear: The only way to break up with "the algorithm" is to leave social media. And also to limit your use of other platforms run by profit-fueled algorithms, including Google, Spotify, Amazon, and a lot of generative AI.

I'm not saying you have to be a purist or a luddite about it. Frankly, it's not easy or fun to let go of the convenience and cleverness of these tools. But we have to be honest about what problems social media algorithms solve. And they're typically not *our* problems. So if we keep turning to them, we're just fodder for other peoples' problems (and profits).

Garbage in, garbage out. And, eventually, we become the garbage.

3

From Economy to Ecology

Since I wrote the last section, I've started asking people what problem they think social media is solving for them. Typically, I get one of two answers: connection or entertainment.

The folks seeking connection on social media want more friends, deeper relationships, or a sense of community. And I find that they are the most disillusioned with the apps. It's become apparent to them that Facebook, Instagram, X, and TikTok are doing more to keep them *from* connecting with their community than to foster a real sense of community. They tell me about how they never see their friends' posts, how hard it is to keep up in DMs, and why social media just isn't as satisfying as it used to be (all things we explored in the last chapter).

In contrast, the folks seeking entertainment on social media are generally pretty satisfied by what they're finding there. TikTok especially is a flood of dopamine-fueled delight designed to pique our attention every few seconds with something new, unique, beautiful, interesting, inspiring, confronting, or even disgusting — depending on how you've fine-tuned your algorithm.

I'm glad that the folks seeking entertainment feel satisfied by social media. Like I wrote in the last section, I think it's important to align the problem, algorithm, and solution in our social media use. So if the problem you're looking to solve is that you want to be entertained, then a tailored algorithm designed to keep you entertained on the app should dovetail with your goal. But returning to our conversation about attention, I think there's a deeper issue within our desire to be constantly entertained that social media is exacerbating, not solving, for us.

Often when we pick up our phone to open TikTok, Instagram, or YouTube, we're seeking entertainment, and underneath that I think we're seeking pleasure, delight, even joy. In my past experience, the first few minutes on TikTok were often full of surprise and delight. I found novelty and newness there that sparked joy and inspired me. But something always happened as I continued my scroll. Rather than my attention being fully captured by a few videos, I could literally feel it glazing over and going numb as I took in more and more and more and more content. When you're given novelty and newness in a constant supply, it just becomes banal again.

This drop-off from intrigue to ennui makes sense if we think about what problem these algorithms are really solving. We may be seeking entertainment, pleasure or joy. But these apps are trying to make money. TikTok, Instagram, and YouTube are only solving for "how can we entertain you?" insofar as that also answers the question "how do we keep you on the app as a passive consumer?" **The pleasure we find on the apps is only a byproduct of these companies' actual end goal of profit.** Or, perhaps, these pleasures are more like the juicy carrot they offer us as they get us to watch ads or make a purchase.

I can clearly remember when I first downloaded TikTok and felt inspired to try out a few of the fun dances I saw there. I made a silly video of sea otters, then one of me dancing around my apartment. My experience felt active and exciting. But I pretty quickly shifted to becoming a passive consumer of other peoples' videos. After a week or so on TikTok, the only "action" I'd ever take was clicking through to buy something.

When I pulled back from the app, I could see how I was being conditioned in real time from producer to consumer — as well as how those were really my only options on TikTok. I could produce. I could consume. Or I could be consumed.

As that became clear, I realized that I had to find my pleasure and joy elsewhere. TikTok was only offering me a few shreds of those feelings and only offering me these shreds in order to get me to do what it wanted. My attention — and my agency — were atrophying every moment I spent there.

FROM PAYING ATTENTION TO GIVING ATTENTION

So far I think we've accomplished two things in this book. First, we've unpacked how understanding attention through an economic framework always limits attention to the realm of production and productivity. *What can attention produce? In the attention economy, only profits for those who capture that attention and sell it to advertisers.* Then we explored how social media and "the algorithm" turn us into passive consumers, stuck in loops of similarity, always churning toward the next purchase. *What can "the algorithm" offer us? Only the opportunity to buy the next thing.*

My hope for those first two chapters was to explain how the two most prominent ways we understand and talk about our experiences online right now — the attention economy and the algorithm — actually keep us trapped in this specific experience of the internet, and, to some degree, force us to understand ourselves only as producers or consumers. **If we accept that we live in an "attention economy" run by "the algorithm," then our options for change are incredibly limited.** On my more cynical days, I think we're just handing our agency over to the apps for good. But I want to make it clear that we don't have to do that.

As I argued in the first chapter, our attention is not a scarce resource. It is an abundant, expanding, quantum way of being in the world. It is a way of tending to things with tenderness.

If we reclaim what we believe attention to be, we can reclaim how we give our attention to things and to each other. That's why, in this book, I've intentionally shifted my language from "paying attention" to "giving attention" as a way of signaling my own shifting understanding of how attention works. I no longer want to "pay" for something with my attention. I want to "give" my attention to the things I'm interested in and care about.

What does that look like? For me, it's been a process of getting off social media and canceling streaming subscriptions. I watch more films and less reality television. I read books again and actively ask people for book recommendations. I send long voice messages to my friends and have lingering phone calls with those who enjoy that. I turn off notifications everywhere I can. I actually go to the improv shows my friends are hosting. And I travel to see the people I love who live far away, leaving my phone in another room as we linger over their dinner tables. This semantic shift from "paying" attention to "giving" attention may not seem that deep, but I've found it can be profound if you let it.

There are times when I feel like I'm still forced to "pay" attention to something. I had to "pay" attention to renewing my passport this year, organizing my taxes, and keeping tabs on the awful things the US government is doing. I still live in an unjust society. I still have to engage with the oppressive state. I still choose to look at the violence of this world with open eyes. But I'm also deeply interrogating what I feel like I "have" to give my attention to and why I feel that way. In the process, I've found that I don't have to pay attention to many things other people tell me I do.

I share all of this to say that reclaiming our attention can be deeply personally satisfying. If our attention is a camera lens, we're widening the aperture and pointing it at things we actually want to see, not simply the flashiest, splashiest thing around. And through practices like Deep Listening, we're able to feel into our mutual entanglement with life and to find a sense of belonging by embedding ourselves in our context.

It's not necessarily easy work, and it can feel challenging or confusing at times. We have to deprogram and detox from the attention economy and "the algorithm." Anyone who's been through rehab, recovery, or a twelve-step program knows that this work is challenging. But it always yields more life.

I believe that reclaiming our attention ultimately feels good. But I also think it does more than just that. It recenters us in our agency: our innate ability to act and make change in our lives. And it reminds us that those lives are entangled in a shared, ecological context.

So in this third and final chapter of the book, I want to turn to "agency" and "ecology" to make sense of a path beyond, alongside, or just different from the attention economy. I'll begin etymologically as I always do, and then offer a step-by-step process for reclaiming your attention and cultivating it like a garden.

AGENCY

The word agency originates from Medieval Latin *agentia* or "ability" and from Latin *ag(ere)* "to do, drive." It evolved from the Proto-Indo-European morpheme *ag* which means to draw out or forth.

If we boil agency down to just our ability to do or to act, then we can find it everywhere around us. But I think it's more interesting to consider agency as intentional actions —

the things we mean to do or choose to do — and how we choose those actions amidst many choices or options. This idea of agency as *acting for a reason* can be traced all the way back to Aristotle and has been heavily theorized in twentieth century philosophy of action.

An important philosophical text in this area is Gertrude Elizabeth Margaret Anscombe's *Intention*, where she explores the relationship between action and intention. She explains that, by doing one thing intentionally, we may do many other things unintentionally. According to her concept of "action under a description," the same behavior can be described in multiple ways, and some of those descriptions might pick out intentional actions while others do not.

For example, as my partner JJ pointed out while editing this book, under the description "commenting on this manuscript," their action was intentional, but under the description "creating a clicking sound that attracts the cat to the keyboard," their action was not intentional. Even though the same action *did* both things.

Understanding agency as intentional action allows us to consider the nuance of where we're acting with agency on social media and where we're not. Where are we making intentional choices to act on the apps? And what unintentional consequences are embedded in those actions? Going further, where do we feel like our agency is limited and only one choice (or no choice) is available? And how do we find a more expansive set of options online or offline?

Thinking of intention first: Social media is rife with unintentional actions, and almost all of them are designed to make money for social media companies. Following Anscombe, you may be intentionally scrolling Instagram to enjoy a few cat videos but unintentionally making money for Meta by pausing on an ad for a cat scratcher. You may believe you're scrolling to be entertained — and you might even be right — but you're also being shaped into a consumer and having your taste altered unintentionally in the process.

Expanding this to consider agency: I believe agency requires intentional action amidst many possible choices. There have to be many options available for us to choose and act freely among them. In other words, we don't have agency if only a choice or two is available to us, even if we're "intentionally" choosing one of those limited options.

The limitation on choice is exactly the danger I explained about your algorithm and "the algorithm." As your algorithm hones in on what you like, it offers you a more and more narrow set of choices. And as "the algorithm" works toward its goal of keeping you on the app, the choices it offers are heavily determined by that aim, rather than being open to what else you might desire.

For example, you may think you're scrolling for cat videos, but there are only certain types of cat videos available, and those will be more and more curated to look exactly like the other cat videos you like, and those videos are only freely available to watch at all because of how many cat scratcher ads can be placed between them. This is how your feed might end up showing an endless scroll of cute orange cats swatting at toys with ads for those exact toys popping up in between each video. And when that happens, your "choice," or intentional action to scroll through cat videos, unintentionally becomes a long march toward the inevitable purchase of that cat toy (or at least the challenge to advertisers to get you to do so).

This is all to say that even those of us who believe we intend to go on social media just to relax, chill or even "numb out" are still subject to the unintentional descriptions of our actions *and* the limited choices of "our algorithms." **The more I read and learn about social media algorithms, the more convinced I become that there's no true choice on these platforms, only the illusion of choice, and thus the illusion of agency.**

Here's the other side of it though — in our overwhelming, oversaturated, overloaded society, being told what to do can feel like a relief. This is the power of User Experience design. An app, website, or digital interface can tell us how to use it and what to do there — implicitly or explicitly. And since we have to make thousands of other decisions every day, it can be comforting to find places where we don't have to decide what to do next. I understand and empathize with the appeal of letting go of the reins for a while.

But I want to distinguish here between predetermined choices and creative constraints. When we're told exactly what to do in a space *(scroll here, like that, comment below)*, our options are specific and few. We have very little agency on social media platforms. But this is different than when we have an expanse of options and we select specific constraints that help us be present and create.

I often think of the difference between tech tools like Asana and Notion here. Asana is a work management platform that guides you through one specific way of organizing tasks, deadlines, and teams for projects. It tells you how to work, so you can accomplish more within its structure. And its early tagline "Work anytime, anywhere with Asana" reeks of productivity culture.

In contrast, Notion is also a work management platform, but every Notion workspace starts with a blank page. It has powerful tools for organizing information and workflows, but it asks the user to decide how to use them. And it bills itself as a "connected workspace," emphasizing the interconnected, contextual nature of the platform.

As I've worked in Notion and taught classes about the platform over the past few years, I've encountered plenty of people who say something like, "I want to use Notion, but I don't know what to do there." Notion templates have proliferated so that users can copy/paste dashboards and workflows without building on their own. I think there's a tension between Notion's insistence on creating your own uses for the app with users' desire to be told what to do and how to work.

This difference between Asana and Notion, for me, is about agency. **Do we want to take on the task of determining what to do and how to work? Or do we want to be told what to do?** Stepping into agency — instead of away from it — requires the former. We have to be willing to do the work of creation — of building, deciding, connecting, and communicating ourselves.

And here's the thing, I know that plenty of people will read this and feel or say something to the extent of, "I'm too tired, too overwhelmed, too busy, and too worn-thin to do any of that." I can empathize with that and see the systemic reasons why we feel that way!

But I think if we want to reclaim our attention and our agency from these apps, then we have to do this work. There's no way around it. Otherwise, we will continue to fall into the "garbage in, garbage out" trap of social media algorithms, *and* we will continue to acquiesce to the "work anytime anywhere" ethos of productivity software. That's the fate of our attention in the attention economy — always, inevitably directed toward doing work so others profit.

But, again, **we don't have to submit to the attention economy. This is why I love creative constraints even as I rage against predetermined choices.** I understand the adage that "you can do anything, just not everything." So what "anything" do I choose? And how do I create a life where I can choose giving attention over paying attention as much as possible?

For me, this has looked like moving to a more rural area where the cost of living is lower so that I don't need to make as much money. It's meant working for myself instead of a traditional employer. It's meant choosing not to have children and deepening my ties with family members I don't always agree with, so we can materially support each other. It's not all fun or cool, and it's definitely not Instagrammable. But it is my choice. These are decisions I'm making from a place of agency, rather than ones that have been forced on me. And they're made within the creative constraints of my material life. I have certain abilities and privileges and not others. I have a certain amount of money and no more. The "anything" I choose is constrained by my physical, emotional, and material realities, but it's not limited by the predetermined options of billionaire tech founders.

Can everyone make the decisions I have? No, of course not. I don't know the specific context or constraints of your life. But I think that most of us grappling with "the algorithm" and reading philosophical manifestos on the attention economy have more room to maneuver than we're willing to admit. It just might require giving up things we're not willing to give up yet.

Stepping off my soapbox a bit, I want to say that I think agency and attention are two sides of the same coin. Looking at the roots of these words, I'm struck by how complementary the motions of attention and agency are. **As we stretch toward something (with our attention), we draw it and ourselves forth (with our agency).** It feels so deeply intertwined.

So here it is — You can't get your attention back from the apps without drawing yourself and your power forth. You have to choose. You have to act. But you don't have to do it alone.

In our neoliberal worldview, being reminded of our agency can make it feel like the whole world rests on our shoulders. But it doesn't. The whole world rests on the whole world's shoulders. Or, rather, the worlds we choose rest on the shoulders of those who choose them. And we do that in context, with others, *ecologically*. So let's explore ecology next.

ECOLOGY

Like "economy," the word "ecology" has the root *oikos* which means household or dwelling. The distinction between them is their other roots — *nomos* and *logos*. *Nomos* is law or convention, while *logos* is simply the study of. There's a more observational nature to *logos* (and thus ecology), where we're studying rather than inventing laws. And the "house" of *oikos* here is construed as the natural world, our planetary dwelling, rather than the nuclear family and its "household."

The difference between *nomos* and *logos* reminds me of the difference I pointed to in the first section between *tendere* and *tenere* (where *tendere* meant "to stretch" and *tenere* meant "to hold"). There's an openness to a stretch that is closed when we hold or grasp something. Just like there is an openness to our attention that is closed when it's honed by the algorithm. And similarly, I think, there's an openness to studying something that is closed when we turn it into a set of laws or conventions. There's something in *logos* that offers an openness that *nomos* doesn't allow.

Our contemporary definition of ecology was coined in 1873 by German zoologist Ernst Haeckel, who defined it as a "branch of science dealing with the relationship of living things to their environments."[34] Haeckel was a follower of Charles Darwin, who understood ecology in terms of *the struggle for existence*. Darwin himself used economic terms for his investigations of the interrelated world, and in the *Origin of Species* he argued that "all organic beings are striving, it may be said, to seize on each place in the economy of nature."[35]

This language always sounds steeped in colonial thinking to me. So I much prefer Robin Wall Kimmerer's indigenous approach to ecology that emphasizes how we are always relational and always in context.

In her profound book *Braiding Sweetgrass*, Kimmerer insists on placing humans within a broader natural, planetary, and cosmic framework. She also distinguishes between teaching or studying ecology and "doing" ecology, or between learning that we are embedded in the world and actually going out to build relationships in and with the world.

To explain her sense of ecology and economy, Kimmerer offers us the example of weaving the Black Ash Basket. I'll quote her here at length, so I can explain how a false basket is woven on social media.

> "The first two rows of the basket are the hardest. On the first go-round, the splint seems to have a will of its own and wants to wander from the over-under rhythm around the circle ... The second row is almost as frustrating; the spacing is all wrong and you have to clamp the weaver in place to get it to stay ... But then there's the third row—my favorite. At this point, the tension of over is balanced by the tension of under, and the opposing forces start to come into balance. The give and

take—reciprocity—begins to take hold and the parts begin to become a whole. The weaving becomes easy as splints fall snugly into place. Order and stability emerge out of chaos. In weaving well-being for land and people, we need to pay attention to the lessons of the three rows. Ecological well-being and the laws of nature are always the first row. Without them, there is no basket *wisgaak gokpenagen*: a black ash basket of plenty. Only if that first circle is in place can we weave the second. The second reveals material welfare, the subsistence of human needs. Economy built upon ecology. But with only two rows in place, the basket is still in jeopardy of pulling apart. It's only when the third row comes that the first two can hold together. Here is where ecology, economics, and spirit are woven together. By using materials as if they were a gift, and returning that gift through worthy use, we find balance." [36]

I love her line "economy built upon ecology." Here it reminds me that our agency is built upon our attention. We can't draw anything forth if we're not stretching toward it. And "having the whole world at our fingertips" actually does nothing for us if we can't feel our feet on the ground.

I think the literal practice and metaphor of weaving the basket also reminds us that there is a sequence to this work. We have to begin with the first row of ecological well-being and the laws of nature. Then we move to material welfare, and on to sacred meaning-making from there.

The basket we're weaving and pouring our attention into on social media lacks the first row. There is no concern for ecological well-being from these platforms, and the only "laws" present are seemingly those of capitalism. Without the first row, social media is a bottomless sieve for our attention; it can't hold anything and thus it can't build things that meet our human needs. We can stretch toward the third row of spirit and reciprocity on social media, but we will literally never get there from the non-existent first row and wobbly second row of the basket.

Kimmerer's example reminds me that we are wrapped up in the attention economy, but we need to return to an attentive ecology. We need to reweave the first row again. It's challenging and unwieldy, but there's no basket without it.

By reclaiming and restoring our attention and turning back toward the world we live in, we can remake our basket. And eventually, we can get to that third row — the circle of spirit, built on the practice of every basket being a gift.

GARDENING OUR ATTENTION

Unlike Robin Wall Kimmerer, I am not an ecologist. In fact, until very recently, I wouldn't have even said I like "the outdoors." But through this work, I've come to think of the natural world as the ground of our creative constraints. Our lives are limited by the length of a lifespan and the laws of nature. But quantum theory helps me remember that time is a fluid, entangled thing. And ecology reminds me that being itself is a fluid, entangled thing.

So I may have been taught that the purpose of my life is to become self-sufficient with a padded-enough bank account that I can take care of anything that comes my way. But I've come to see how that literally goes against the realities of time and space. We cannot be self-sufficient. On the most fundamental level, we are all intertwined. This is where the title of this book comes from:

Your attention is sacred, because your life is sacred.

Your attention is sacred, because your time is sacred.

Your attention is sacred, because it's your portal to our glorious entanglement.

This reminds me of the question Jenny Odell poses in her book *Saving Time*: "Would it be possible not to save and spend time but to garden it — by saving, inventing, and stewarding different rhythms of life?"[37] She poses this question hypothetically, but I want to ask and answer it here:

Would it be possible not to pay attention but to give it?

How do we garden our attention?

How can we steward different rhythms of life?

Throughout this book, I proposed answers to these questions that range from listening to the radio to calling your friends to leaving social media. I also invited us to consider the value of creative constraints and the freedom of starting with a blank page or the first row of the basket.

But can we weave that into a methodology or a step-by-step process? Because it's one thing to acknowledge that our attention is not an economic resource, or to believe that it's inherently linked to our agency, or maybe even to desire to step back or away from social media as a result. But how do we really reclaim our attention, nurture our agency, and rebuild community alongside or away from the apps?

I'd like to propose we garden our attention and quite literally treat our attention like a garden. I'm only an amateur gardener, but I've picked up a few things in my years of tending to my raised beds. I've also found ways to map those lessons onto my experience of life, love, and community.

So after many pages of critical analysis, I now offer you a gentle method. One that insists that **attention is not a scarce resource to be distributed but a rich terrain to be treasured and cultivated.** Here are five principles for where we might begin gardening our attention:

Principle One: Explore what's already present

As a new gardener, I thought that gardening began when I ordered my seed packets, poked around the local hardware shop, and bought a few seedlings. But I've since learned that growing a flourishing garden requires starting with the soil.

We need to explore what kind of earth is present, what nutrients are there (or not), what's already growing and what pests are present — including if those pre-existing plants or pests might help or harm what we desire to grow. It's rather obvious when I think about it, but gardening begins with attention to what is already present.

So, if I'm gardening my attention itself, I'd begin by noticing what I'm already noticing. I might try out an attention audit where I spend a few days or a week carrying a small notebook (or a phone note) around with me and jotting down what sparks my interest and what takes up my time. I'd make notes not only on what I was paying attention to but also how it felt to attend to those things.

This isn't a scientific (or Taylorist) exercise, meaning it's not intended to be a second-by-second accounting of your day, and it should go beyond simple time tracking or "screen-time" calculations. It's meant to help you begin to tap into not only the objects of your attention but also the impact those objects have on your attention — not only what you are doing, but also how it makes you feel.

Here's an example of what a simple version of this could look like from one of my recent mornings:

Wake up and immediately pick up my phone — start scrolling email and feel stressed — swipe over to YouTube and start watching videos, at first I feel calm then I begin to feel numb, I can tell I'm swiping compulsively from video to video, am I even paying attention to these things?

Get up and go downstairs for a 20-minute bike ride — while I'm on the stationary bike it's all I can pay attention to. Interesting how physical activity requires my full attention.

Take a quick shower, thinking about work the whole time, so once I get dressed I go to my computer, open my email and begin replying to things. I meant to spend about 10 minutes on email, but when I look up it's been an hour. I notice that email took over my attention, and that ... doesn't feel good. I don't like when I get so "reactive" rather than proactive with how I spend my work time. Now I'm an hour into work and feel like I haven't gotten anything done.

I have a work meeting and notice that I spend half of it covertly checking my email and other notifications during the meeting. I wonder what a meeting that took my full attention would look like? What would we do? How long would it be? How would that feel? Would I like it or hate it?

Meeting's over. Now I'm hungry, but I ignore that to do a quick task for a client. This ends up taking 30 minutes and I'm starving by the time I finish. I'm tempted to continue ignoring that, but I decide to get up and eat. I go into the kitchen and open the fridge, which is immediately overwhelming, so I close it. I don't know what to do with all the food in there, and I'm too hungry to make a plan. My attention feels ... scattered and shut down. I grab a granola bar from the pantry and eat that as I go back to work.

Once you've completed an attention audit like this, I'd invite you to go back through it for clues of your various attention triggers or balms, or — to use our garden metaphor —

your pests and nutrients. Here are a few things I notice from my narrative, to help you decipher yours:

First, I notice that picking up my phone right when I wake up is something I do every day, but it never feels good. I often create stress by looking at email that I then immediately want to numb by opening an app like YouTube. This "attention – stress – numb out" cycle is one that I slip into so easily on my phone, and something that I'd like to "weed out" as I tend to my attention garden.

Next, it's interesting that my stationary bike rides are moments where I feel like something has my "full attention." I have my phone and my iPad in front of me on my bike, so tech is present but it has a specific, singular purpose, and the movement of my body keeps me from using the tech for anything else. Sometimes my mind will "wander" during a bike ride, but my body pulls me back to the present moment. This is definitely something to explore more as I garden my attention.

My questions about meetings are also interesting clues for ways I might tend to my attention and shift my workflow to suit it. And while I know that I often override my body's signals for hunger and thirst (a habit I do hope to amend), there's also something to be noticed in how opening the fridge actually shuts down my desire for food rather than nourishing it. These are more clues for how I can garden my attention in the future.

Completing an attention audit is how I develop awareness around the objects of my attention and how they impact the quality of my attention. From that awareness, I may decide to make some changes, but before we move on to shifting our behaviors, there's one more important piece of the attention audit that I haven't mentioned yet: weather and climate.

In gardening, this is the meteorological weather: How much sun do you get? How much rain? When does the frost typically begin or end each year? In our attention audit, we can approach this in terms of our emotional and material weather. Thinking materially first: How much stress are you under right now? How well are you fed? Are you taking care of your basic needs for water and rest? Do you have money to meet your needs? Do you feel financially stable or secure? And then emotionally: Do you feel supported by your friends or family? Are you in the middle of any complicated interpersonal dynamics? Are there others that rely on you for day-to-day care? Does your job feel like it builds you up or tears you down each day?

The answers to these questions provide clues for how well-resourced you are on many levels of your life. And I think they're important to ask at the beginning of our attention-gardening, because gardening in the arctic tundra is very different from gardening on a temperate flood-plain. It's helpful to recognize (and reckon with) our starting point, before we move right to trying to plant some tomatoes.

Principle Two: Start small

Most gardening guides I've read will encourage you to begin your garden with just a few plants. They'll also often advise beginning with a container garden or raised bed where you can (to some extent) have more control over your plot.

I think the same is true when we garden our attention. We can begin with the most manageable container and the thing that can always grow. For me and my garden, this initially meant planting a single raised bed with radishes in early spring. For me and my attention, this initially meant setting aside an hour each week to read a romance novel. No matter how busy, scattered, or unfocused I felt in any given week, I could always find an hour to immerse myself in a book.

The key to starting small with your attention garden is setting aside a manageable amount of time to do an activity that you genuinely enjoy. It can begin with five minutes and a paintbrush. Or a 15-minute walk without your phone. Tending to your attention is not about forcing yourself to do things, or about slotting an hour onto your calendar for activities you feel like you "should" be completing each week. This isn't a matter of compulsion, it's a matter of choice. It's not about discipline, it's about pleasure.

As you step deeper into that practice of pleasure by giving your attention fully to something you enjoy, little-by-little your attentive capacity expands. You create time for a 30-minute walk rather than find time for a 15-minute one. You read for three hours instead of one. You "lose track" of time doing something you love on a weekend afternoon, rather than rushing from one obligation to the next.

With starting small, I also like to invite myself to explore containers where there are rules or norms about "paying attention." For instance, I love going to a movie theater rather than watching a film at home because, in the theater, I have to give my full attention to the movie. I can't pull out my phone, and I never have to get up to let the dog out. Sometimes the movie draws me in and time flies, while other times it doesn't and my hours there drag. But, either way, I've practiced giving my attention to art and nothing else for a small period of time. And I'm able to gently notice what that experience felt like.

Here are a few things to consider in your own practice of starting small while attention gardening: Is there an hour or a set time each week where you can practice giving your attention to something you want to tend to? What are a few things you want to give your attention to? How can you add them to your life? How can you cultivate a practice of giving your attention by choice, before you begin trying to change any self-perceived "bad habits"?

Principle Three: Be intentional, then let go of control

Once we've practiced small acts of giving attention, our work can expand beyond those specific containers. This is where we begin to cultivate our attention garden in its many forms. We not only seed the radishes each spring. We also grow lettuce, tomatoes, fruit trees, and flowers all summer and into the fall.

I think of my attention as the fertile earth of my consciousness and my gardening practice as how I intentionally point that consciousness toward the things I care about and tend to them. So some days I'm pointing myself toward my email inbox and other days I'm taking myself to the movies. Some days I'm able to relish in exactly the things I care about while, on other days, I have to give my attention to things I wish I didn't have to notice anymore.

Gardening happens over seasons and years, not single days or moments. So for me, I cherish my time with my spring radishes and summer tomatoes, but I also still water the crab grass even though I know I'll replace it with native plants one day. Some years I try my hardest to grow basil from seed, and it never works. Others my lettuce rots because we get too much rain. I give my attention to these "failed" experiments and learn things about myself in the process. Just like you might still spend time scrolling social media even as you rejuvenate your offline interests and break up with "the algorithm" in your own time.

So attention gardening has two sides. We have to be intentional and thoughtful in how and where we give our attention. But we also have to recognize that we're not a purely free agent acting independently of the world around us.

As much care and intention as we pour into our attention gardening, our garden is one part of a larger ecosystem. It's inherently connected to the planet, and it's subject to the local fauna and weather of our bioregion. We can plant intentionally, but we can't control what grows successfully in any given season (or ever). Similarly, we may have a lot of obligations that require or demand our attention, leaving us relatively little time to tend to the things we choose. Or we may have relatively few obligations and realize that we're filling our time with things we don't care about, when we really do have the capability of cultivating a grand garden this year. We may live in a region with poor soil and very little rain. Or we may live in a lush floodplain where the native plants can feed us and almost everything else grows abundantly.

As you practice gardening your attention, I invite you to remember both sides of this metaphor: that you can choose what you plant and what you water, but you can't control the weather or what's capable of growing in the climate where you live. Analogously, you can choose what you give your attention to, but other things around you will still demand your attention sometimes.

You also can't garden the whole world. *Your* garden delineates the part of the world that you've committed to tending to. It's the shifting scope of your attention and the natural landscape of your one wild and precious life.

So what are the things you care about and want to plant in your garden? What native plants can you learn to embrace? What others can you seed and tend to? How much space do you have this season? And how can you shift with the weather patterns as needed?

Remember: Gardening is about intention and surrender. We make choices, but we don't seek control.

Principle Four: Embrace biodiversity and seasonal rhythms

One of the most devastating impacts of industrial farming has been the introduction and establishment of monocropping. Monocropping is the practice of growing a single crop, repeatedly, year after year on the same land. While it maximizes profits for some farmers, it has devastating impacts on the soil, depleting it of nutrients and making it susceptible to pests and diseases.

I don't think it's a stretch to say that spending all our time scrolling social media feeds is a form of monocropping our attention. While it may feel like you're seeing a lot of different things on social media, the format, pace, and algorithmic curation of those things makes them all blend together as they speed by. On the apps, we all become harvesters and sprayers travelling the field/feed.

Now, I'm not saying this to critique farmers. I know many of them refuse to grow in this way and that even those who do monocrop often have deep connections to the land they tend. But I use the example of monocropping to argue that we need more diversity in our attention gardens, just like we do in natural ecosystems.

If you're interested in spending less time scrolling on social media, I'd like to suggest you replace the time spent scrolling not with one other thing you now do a lot more, but with many things you do for different durations of time and depths of experience. An hour on TikTok can be turned into an hour reading a book. But it can also be a fifteen-minute walk, ten minutes of putting away dishes, thirty minutes revising the essay you've been writing, and five minutes drinking a glass of water.

Diversifying our attention ecosystem also requires diversifying our tools. I see people praising the all-in-one nature of social media apps (and other online tools) for how much they can do for us. For instance, Facebook is a place to connect with friends, watch funny videos, buy a mini-fridge, sell your old bike, scope out local events, and even watch the news. But what if the all-in-one-ness is itself part of the problem? When Meta or Google solve all our problems, then we're only getting their approach to problem-solving. And as I've shown here, their approaches to problem-solving all start to look like increased time spent scrolling and increased money spent on sponsored products.

Like any healthy ecosystem, our attention gardens need to be diverse. And we cultivate biodiversity by planting a variety of things in a variety of ways and giving our attention to all of them. Rather than seeing diversity and multiplicity as a problem, we have to see it as a gift. As Audre Lorde reminds us in "Difference and Survival," "The house of your difference is the longing for your greatest power and your deepest vulnerability. It is an indelible part of your life's arsenal."[38]

When I think of the role of difference in attention gardening, I think it has to do with the different seeds we plant, the different tools we use, *and* the different phases of growth over time. Gardens have seasonal rhythms. Planting in spring, tending in summer, harvesting in fall, and resting in winter. Similarly, our attention has rhythms as well. Part of embracing biodiversity in our attention gardening is also embracing the varying depths of our attention and the varying modes of attention between us. Sometimes we may want to "lose track" of time while other times we may relish in giving our attention to multiple things at once or in zoning out and seemingly giving attention to nothing. Additionally, what it looks like when I give my attention to something will surely look different than what it looks like when you do.

So what are your inner rhythms? When do you have more energy or attention throughout your days, weeks, months or years? And how can you ensure you're not replacing the monocrop of social media with another monocrop? Where do you embrace diversity in your garden? How do you invite differences while steering yourself toward pleasure and care?

Principle Five: Linger with what's regenerative

My final principle for attention gardening comes from what I've learned about bulbs. When I was a kid, my dad planted a bunch of irises around our house. Back then, I was thoroughly unimpressed when we put these plants in the ground. To me, they were just boring, brown, dirty, squishy blobs that I had to spend a whole day digging holes for. But a few months later, I was surprised when green leaves sprouted up where those blobs had gone in the ground. And then I was amazed when those leaves turned into gorgeous flowers in a rainbow of colors. I figured my dad would be making me plant bulbs again a few months after that, but I was pleased when that didn't happen, and I was absolutely *shocked* when the flowers grew and bloomed again the next year without any extra work from us!

In case you, like me, had no idea why this happened: Bulbs are a resting stage of a plant that lives underground. Common with lilies, tulips, and onions, bulbs can be planted once and will grow back for years to come as long as the soil and rain stay healthy over time.

My experience with bulbs taught me that the ratio between hard work and outcome isn't as direct as I thought it was. Life, in fact, is not an hourly job. There is no wage for staying alive day after day or salary that computes my contributions to the world versus the effort I put in. Additionally, "how much time" something takes can feel incredibly different based on how much I enjoy doing that thing or reaping the results of it.

This is a lesson I'm constantly learning as an artist and business owner. Doing things I don't want to do takes so much more energy and effort than doing things I want to do — even if those things take exactly the same amount of time. For instance, an hour spent compiling tax forms feels way more draining to me than an hour spent talking to a client. It's important to notice this in the process, and then also to look to the future. Because while I may not relish in compiling the tax forms, the savings I get from doing so may allow me to spend even fewer hours talking to clients next year, and that might feel like the biggest win of all!

When we're gardening our attention, I think it's important to take time to notice not only how things feel in the moment (which is important!) but also to consider which actions are regenerative and provide more energy over time without additional effort on our part. This is the real key to a thriving garden — noticing what works together and has impacts that last over time.

So what are the things you pay attention to that give you more energy, rather than less? Do you finish an hour spent scrolling on social media feeling more alive than when you started? For me, the answer to that was a definitive NO. But I do feel more alive when I finish reading a book. That story might fuel me for days or weeks to come as I revisit my memories of it, tell others about it, and even create my own art from it.

All of this is a reminder that attention gardening may feel strenuous at first, because it's hard work to repair the damage done by monocropping our minds on social media!

But the farther away I get from my time on social media, the more I see the fruits of my attention-gardening labors. I'm not starting from scratch anymore, and in fact there are so many bulbs that return year after year as long as I notice them. They're the seasonal rituals I do, the treasured stories I share, the beloved people I visit, and the deep relationships we form. All of these bring me a deep, lasting pleasure that I never found on social media. They remind me that *my attention is sacred.*

Conclusion

I have seen time and time again in my personal life — and with the thousands of people I've spoken to about social media — that these apps are doing immeasurable harm to our attention and our agency.

If you're reading this, I think you probably knew that even before you opened this book. But I hope that what I've written here has shown you how and why this is happening, and that it has invited you to consider ways that you might slow or stop this process.

As I conclude, I want to be clear that I understand that social media algorithms are not the only problematic forces in our world. Most of us live under racist, sexist, oppressive regimes, and we battle discrimination and violence regularly. We can't choose where we're born or the global conditions of the planet when we arrive here. But I believe that we can choose how much time (if any) we spend on social media.

And while I also understand that social media has been a portal for so many people to dream beyond the harsh and uninhabitable conditions of their daily lives, there is always a trade-off — or even an inherent impossibility, as Audre Lorde reminds us — of trying to use the master's tools to dismantle the master's house.

This book is intended as a rallying cry for more of us to reclaim our attention and our agency from social media. To spend less or no time on these apps. To refuse to step into their producer/consumer cycles. To stop having our taste honed into oblivion by an algorithm. To realize that our impulse to numb out every negative feeling by scrolling is actually harmful, and not, in fact, a funny joke.

This book is also a gentle reminder that we each do this work in our own way and at our own pace. As I'm always saying on *Off the Grid*, I'm not here to judge you, just to remind you of your options. I want you to begin tending to your attention garden and to plant seeds of pleasure, joy, and community there. I also want to make sure you don't forget —

Your attention is sacred *except on social media.*

So Now You Want to Leave Social Media?

As I wrote throughout this book, *Your Attention is Sacred* is not an attempt to convince you that you should leave social media. I think that's a very personal decision we each have to make on our own.

But if you've made it to the end of this book and you find yourself looking around and asking something like, *"Okay well now I want to leave social media... so how do I do that?"* — I have two resources for you.

The first is a five-step plan for leaving any social platform and the second is my list of 100 ways to share your work and life off social media. I've been sharing these tools for years in my free Leaving Social Media Toolkit (which you can download at offthegrid.fun/toolkit). I wanted to include them here as well to make it just a little bit easier for you to put this book into practice.

I hope these resources can support you wherever you might be in your journey with social media.

5-step Plan for Leaving Social Media

U se these five steps and the reflection questions below to make your plan for leaving any social media platform.

Step 1: Decide that you're going to leave and when

This is the biggest step, and it takes time. In fact, it might take years of wanting to leave social media before you actually exit the platform. *That is okay!* There is no rush. I recommend reflecting on the following questions while you're moving through your decision-making.

Reflection questions:

- Why do I want to leave social media?
- What am I afraid I'll lose when I leave social media?
- What do I hope I'll gain when I leave social media?
- Which platforms do I want to leave?
- How long do I want to leave for?
- Do I need to consider my relationships, personal sharing practice, or business when I leave?
- When is a good time for me to leave? Is there a particular season, phase in my cycle or the moon's cycle, or time of year that would make this easier for me?
- What's a leaving date I want to make a soft commitment to?

Step 2: Announce your exit and share how people can stay in touch

My number one rule for leaving social media is: *don't ghost your community*. Whether you're connecting with friends, followers, customers, or clients on the apps, you want to tend to those relationships as you make your exit. Giving them somewhere else to connect with you could look like starting an email list, reminding them of your website, or sharing your phone number with close friends so you can text.

Remember: community care is key! And leaving social media doesn't have to mean losing touch with your friends and fans. To help with this process I recommend reflecting on the following questions.

Reflection questions:

- What other platforms will I use instead of social media?
- How can my friends, community, clients, or customers keep in touch with me and learn about my life and work in the future?
- How much time will my community need in order to learn that I'm leaving and to follow me off social?

Step 3: Request your data from the platform and archive it offline

If you've been sharing your life and work on social media, you might have a lot of data on these platforms! In the process of leaving, it's important to collect that data and store it offline or in other online spaces.

Archiving your information is the only way you'll have a record of all the statuses you posted on Facebook, photos you shared on Instagram, or quippy thoughts you tweeted. It's also a good way to understand exactly what information that platform has collected about you and to request deletion where desired. Here are a few reflection questions to guide you through this process.

Reflection questions:

- What platforms are you leaving? What data have you shared on that platform, and will the platform let you request a copy of your data?
- Is there anything else you want to capture or save from that platform?
- Is there anything you want to delete or archive before you leave?

Step 4: Change your profile to share that you're no longer on the platform and how to reach you

When you leave a social media platform, you need to decide if you're keeping your profile up (but no longer logging in), deactivating (so you can return in the future), or deleting your profile entirely (and erasing yourself from that space).

If you're leaving your profiles online, you'll want to clearly signal that you're no longer active on that platform. The questions below help you consider how to do that.

Reflection questions:

- Will your profile stay online after you leave the platform, or will you be taking it down when you leave?
- If your profile stays up, how will people know you're not active there when you're gone?
- What resources, links, or autoresponders do you want in place for anyone who comes across your profile in the future?

Step 5: Sign off!

Our fifth and final step is to sign off of social media! When the day comes to make your final post and log off for the last time or delete your account, I highly recommend planning something sweet and ceremonial for yourself.

Maybe you host a funeral for your TikTok account, or soak in the tub as you archive every last Instagram post, or burn a transcript of your Twitter profile.

However you sign off, make it a ritual that feels meaningful to you. You deserve it.

100 Ways to Share Your Work/Life Off Social Media

When I decided to leave Instagram, I knew that I didn't want to quit sharing my life and work — I just wanted to do it somewhere other than social media. So in the process of leaving social platforms, I challenged myself to come up with as many ways to share what I'm up to in my personal life and my business as I could. And thus, this list was born!

Below I've brainstormed 100 ways to share your work and life that aren't social media. Some things on this list are about making friends. Others are about getting new clients. Some entries are about getting clear on what sharing means to or requires from you. And some are just for fun!

I hope this list can inspire you in your own journey divesting from social media. *Enjoy!*

1. Start an email newsletter.
2. Send a postcard.
3. Call your friends and family.
4. Create or update your website.
5. Start a blog.
6. Put up a flyer at a local coffee shop.
7. Join a Discord server.
8. Launch a podcast.
9. Make stickers and stick them all over town.

10. Find your local community college and see what continuing education courses or networking meetups they host.
11. Take a workshop and tell people what you do when you introduce yourself.
12. Join a pen pal exchange.
13. Sign up to write letters to someone who's incarcerated.
14. Make a zine.
15. Host a workshop at a favorite local or virtual spot.
16. Try out a community app like Geneva or Clubhouse.
17. Ship a care package.
18. Put a sign in your window.
19. Put a sign in your yard.
20. Volunteer your expertise to a non-profit or mutual aid project.
21. Write a fan letter or email to your fave artist, author, podcaster, or local government official.
22. Invite someone for (virtual) coffee.
23. Learn about and implement SEO so people actually see your website.
24. Pitch an article about your work to a journalist or publication.
25. Set up a calendar link so people can easily book time to chat with you.
26. Write a book.
27. Host a book club.
28. Make a playlist.
29. Set up a group text.
30. Let your alumnae association know what you've been up to.

31. Place an ad on a radio station.
32. Place an ad in a magazine.
33. Hell, place an ad on a billboard!
34. Write an op-ed for the local newspaper.
35. Create your own newspaper and put it in Free Little Libraries around town.
36. Ask a local business if you can put up a flyer or leave business cards by their register.
37. See what's happening at your local library or rec center and show up for a community gathering.
38. Host your own online community on a platform like MightyNetworks.
39. Schedule a weekly friend date or open "office hours" for virtual or IRL hangs.
40. Write an essay for an online or print publication.
41. Pitch yourself as a guest for a podcast.
42. Ask a friend to share your work with their community.
43. Collaborate with a friend or colleague on an event or offering.
44. Leave reviews for businesses, podcasts, and books you love.
45. Ask customers, clients, or admirers to leave you reviews.
46. Create a yearbook or annual report.
47. Develop an app.
48. Create a magazine.
49. Host a webinar.
50. Stand outside and shout to the sky.
51. Rent a booth at a local craft fair, business fair, farmers market, or trade show.

52. Create or update your business cards.
53. Join a local coworking space.
54. Two words: bumper stickers.
55. Two more words: graphic tees.
56. Two final words: fanny packs.
57. Ask everyone you know to tell one other person about your work.
58. Send holiday cards.
59. Make some funny memes.
60. Hang out on a livestreaming platform like Twitch.
61. Read or write fanfiction for your favorite series.
62. Hang out at a local coffee shop — or bookstore, bakery, or bar — and befriend the babes who work there.
63. Send valentines.
64. Host a fundraiser for a favorite local organization.
65. Start a Free Little Library, Pantry, or Love Fridge with your neighbors.
66. Share some of your photos, sounds, or words with a Creative Commons license for free use by others.
67. Go to a virtual conference and actively participate.
68. Put up flyers on the street corners around where you live.
69. Practice telling people who you are. Record an audio note of yourself saying it over and over again. Write it down 10 or 100 times.
70. Practice telling people how they can work with you. Record an audio note of yourself saying it over and over again. Write it down 10 or 100 times.
71. Create a free presentation about something you're good at, and share it so others can learn from you.

72. Spend time writing or speaking about your ideal client or friend. Imagine them into existence.
73. Go for a walk and look around.
74. Take a drive and look around.
75. Buy domain names for popular things you do, and reroute them to your website.
76. Reconsider what you really want to share.
77. Reconsider who you really want to share with.
78. Write yourself a theme song.
79. Invest in a session with a healer or coach you admire.
80. Put all your info and links in your email signature.
81. Use a service like Flodesk to set up a free download that you share with people who join your email list.
82. Drink something warm and care for your voice.
83. Make a list of people who do similar things as you, and reach out to see if you can collaborate on something.
84. Make a list of people who do way different things than you, and reach out to see if you can collaborate.
85. Make a media kit.
86. Take new headshots or promo photos you love.
87. Create a Discord or Slack server for your community.
88. Launch a course on a searchable platform like Teachable or Skillshare.
89. Host a game night or online trivia.
90. Create a useful tool or template using a service like Notion or Airtable, and send it to everyone you think might appreciate it.
91. Chalk the sidewalk.
92. Commission a mural.
93. Write a guest post for a friend or colleague's blog.

94. Film a commercial (for TV or just for your website).
95. Make a giant sign and hire a sign-spinner (or do it yourself!).
96. Reach out to one new person a day for a whole month.
97. Reconnect with one person you already know each day for a whole month.
98. Take a deep breath. Then another one. And another one.
99. Actually do something (or a lot of things) on this list.
100. Write your own list of 100 ways to share!

References

Every book is a web of all the texts the writer has read — the poems that inspired them, the podcast episodes that engaged them, the books that educated them, and every person they encountered along the journey to their printed pages.

As a former academic, I believe in the importance of citation, and I especially heed Dr. Sara Ahmed's call to citation as a feminist practice. Below I've listed all of the published books that I referenced in *Your Attention is Sacred*, as well a few that inspired me but were not directly quoted in these pages. Following the reference list, you'll find the notes cited throughout the text.

Bowler, Maria. *Making Time: A New Vision for Crafting a Life beyond Productivity*. Baker Books, 2025.

Byrd, Rudolph P., Johnnetta Betsch Cole, and Beverly Guy-Sheftall, eds. *I am your sister: Collected and unpublished writings of Audre Lorde*. Oxford University Press, 2009.

Chayka, Kyle. *Filterworld: How Algorithms Flattened Culture*. Doubleday, 2024.

Davenport, Thomas H. and John C. Beck. *The Attention Economy: Understanding the New Currency of Business*. Harvard Business School Press, 2001.

Kimmerer, Robin Wall. *Braiding Sweetgrass*. Milkweed Editions, 2013.

Lanier, Jaron. *Ten Arguments for Deleting Your Social Media Accounts Right Now*. Henry Holt and Company, 2018.

Louridas, Panos. *Algorithms*. MIT Press, 2020.

Mbiti, John S. *African Religions and Philosophy (2nd ed.)*. Heinemann, 1990.

Noble, Safiya Umoja. *Algorithms of Oppression: How Search Engines Reinforce Racism.* NYU Press, 2018.

Odell, Jenny. *How to Do Nothing: Resisting the Attention Economy.* Melville House Publishing, 2019.

Odell, Jenny. *Saving Time: Discovering a Life Beyond the Clock.* Random House, 2023.

Oliveros, Pauline. *Quantum Listening.* Spiral House and Silver Press, 2024.

Phillips, Rasheedah. *Dismantling the Master's Clock: On Race, Space, and Time.* AK Press, 2025.

Wynn-Williams, Sarah. *Careless People: A Cautionary Tale of Power, Greed, and Lost Idealism.* Flatiron Books, 2025.

NOTES

1. The notes in this book include both citations and observations in an informal style. You can view the full references for any books cited in the reference list above.

2. All etymology references in this book were sourced from etymonline.com.

3. Notably this root *ten* produced two different Latin verbs: *tendere*, meaning "to stretch," and *tenere*, meaning "to hold, grasp." This suggests we might find a slight difference in words that originate in the stretch of *tendere* (like tender and attention) and words deriving from the grasp of *tenere* (like tenacity or contain). The openness of a stretch compared to the close-fistedness of a hold is something we'll return to at the end of the book.

4. This combines a few entries from the Merriam Webster, Oxford, and Cambridge dictionaries.

5. This definition comes from William James' book, *The Principles of Psychology*, which was published in 1890. I first found it through Maria Popova of *The Marginalian* at themarginalian.org/2016/03/25/william-james-attention.

6. My dissertation was titled *Toward Feminist Aesthetics: Feminist Provocations to German Idealist Aesthetics*. You can access it through the DePaul University Library at via.library.depaul.edu/etd/296.

7. I first learned this quotation from Maria Popova of *The Marginalian*. She attributes it to Weil's *First and Last Notebooks* which were published in 1970 and are now out of print. You can find Popova's citation at themarginalian.org/2015/08/19/simone-weil-attention-gravity-and-grace.

8. This definition comes from the Oxford English Dictionary, which is integrated with Google Search.

9. Found at bea.gov/resources/learning-center/what-to-know-gdp in Spring 2025.

10. This statement was found at aeaweb.org/resources/students/what-is-economics in Spring 2025.

11. It's interesting to track how the relationship between knowledge and power shifts as this happens. Knowledge may still be power, but that power is now in the hands of those who can best parse this glut of information, rather than the select few who possess the information at all. Think of the thousands of pages of top-secret information publicly available thanks to Julian Assange and WikiLeaks and how ill-equipped most of us are to do anything with this information.

12. Thomas H. Davenport and John C. Beck. *The Attention Economy: Understanding the New Currency of Business*. Page 2.

13. For more on how Taylorism functions in Amazon warehouses, I recommend reading this study: "Coercion, Consent, and Class Consciousness: How Workers Respond to Amazon's Production Regime." Vallas, S. P., & Kronberg, A. *Socius, 9*. 2023.

14. Pauline Oliveros. *Quantum Listening*. Page 52.

15. I'd like to add a note here that may be a slight diversion. I think what I'm describing with my experience of Quantum Listening could be compared to what Mihaly Csikszentmihalyi calls a "flow state," where one experiences full immersion and ecstasy with a task at hand. (Watch his TED talk called

Flow, The Secret to Happiness for an explanation.) I appreciate Csikszentmihalyi's work, but I'm wary of two things. One is how Csikszentmihalyi bases his argument in how many "bits" of information humans process in a flow state versus in other states. As I've explained here, I don't think measuring attention by counting information processed is a viable path. My second hesitation is about how I see "flow states" used by many attention theorists. On my reading, writers like Chris Hayes and Johann Hari seem to valorize the flow state as the antithesis to — and cure for — the fragmentation of our attention on social media. In contrast, I think that glorifying any one way of thinking, being, or attending to the world is a mistake (and also a rather ableist move that dismisses neurodivergence). The beauty of attention is like the beauty of humanity: it lies within its diversity of forms. Quantum Listening and/or flow states are one form of attention. I believe they can help us break free from the false belief that clock-time is reality, but they shouldn't be measured or elevated as better than any other forms of attention.

16.   John S. Mbiti. *African Religions and Philosophy (2nd ed.).* Page 17.

17.   Rasheedah Phillips. *Dismantling the Master's Clock: On Race, Space, and Time.* Page 1.

18.   Maria Bowler. *Making Time: A New Vision for Crafting a Life beyond Productivity.* Page 37.

19.   This might be the place to note that I have a pretty broad definition of social media that includes many apps that others might not put in this category, like Pinterest. I think there are meaningful differences between Facebook and Pinterest, but I also see very similar algorithmic logics and monetization methods at play on their platforms. In this manifesto, I move fluidly between critiques of Facebook, Instagram, Tiktok, Pinterest, YouTube, Google and other platforms, but I often unpack their nuances on my podcast.

20.   Safiya Umoja Noble. *Algorithms of Oppression: How Search Engines Reinforce Racism.* Page 4.

21.   "Unpacking the Social Dilemma — Alignment & Algorithms with Vickie Curtis." *Off the Grid*. 7/20/2022.

22.   Jaron Lanier. *Ten Arguments for Deleting Your Social Media Accounts Right Now*. Pages 5-7.

23.   From *Capital One Shopping Research,* accessed at capitaloneshopping.com/research/instagram-shopping-statistics and capitaloneshopping.com/research/tiktok-shopping-statistics in Spring 2025.

24.   A few studies pointing to this include: "Irritability and Social Media Use in US Adults." Perlis RH, Uslu A, Schulman J, et al. *JAMA Netw Open*. 2025.; "Social Media and Mental Health" Braghieri, L, and Levy, Ro'ee and Makarin, Alexey. *SSRN*. 2022.; "Association Between Social Media Use and Depress Among U.S. Young Adults" Lin LY, Sidani JE, Shensa A, Radovic A, Miller E, Colditz JB, Hoffman BL, Giles LM, Primack BA. *Depress Anxiety*. 2016.

25.   "Getting Out of Your Algorithm — with Kate Smalley." *Off the Grid*. 10/9/2024.

26.   Jenny Odell. *How to Do Nothing: Resisting the Attention Economy*. Page 136.

27.   Jenny Odell. *How to Do Nothing: Resisting the Attention Economy*. Page 136-7.

28.   Jaron Lanier. *Ten Arguments for Deleting Your Social Media Accounts Right Now*. Pages 14-15.

29.   Jaron Lanier. *Ten Arguments for Deleting Your Social Media Accounts Right Now*. Page 16.

30.   Panos Louridas. *Algorithms*. Page 76.

31.   Jaron Lanier. *Ten Arguments for Deleting Your Social Media Accounts Right Now*. Pages 6-7.

32.   Safiya Umoja Noble. *Algorithms of Oppression: How Search Engines Reinforce Racism*. Page 36.

33.   Safiya Umoja Noble. *Algorithms of Oppression: How Search Engines Reinforce Racism*. Page 36.

34.   Haeckel wrote in German, so I learned this from the Environment and Society Portal at environmentandsoci-

ety.org/tools/
keywords/ernst-haeckel-coins-term-oecologia-or-ecology

35. This is available to read online for free at darwin-on-line.org.uk/Variorum

36. Robin Wall Kimmerer. *Braiding Sweetgrass*. Pages 152-3.

37. Jenny Odell. *Saving Time: Discovering a Life Beyond the Clock*. Page 224.

38. Rudolph P. Byrd, Johnnetta Betsch Cole, and Beverly Guy-Sheftall, eds. *I am your sister: Collected and unpublished writings of Audre Lorde*. Pages 201-205.

Acknowledgments

This book would not exist without the contributions of every guest and listener of *Off the Grid* podcast. Thank you for tuning in, sharing your experiences, joining me in conversation, and supporting me in this work.

I also want to thank all of my dearest biz friends, especially Kening Zhu for reading an early draft of this manuscript and Nic Antoinette and Taylor Elyse Morrison for listening to many voice messages full of stress and excitement as the book came to life.

My biggest thanks goes to my partner JJ, who read this book many times while editing the manuscript for me. And to my elderly Pekingese pup Zoe who napped (and snored) sweetly next to my desk while I typed away each day. Also thanks to my cat Wilco for swatting at my fingertips and reminding me to step away from the computer. The three of you are my family. I love you.

ABOUT THE AUTHOR

Amelia Hruby is a feminist writer and podcaster with a PhD in philosophy from DePaul University. Over the past decade, she's been a college professor, a community organizer, and a radio DJ.

Now, she is the founder of Softer Sounds podcast studio and the host of the popular podcast *Off the Grid: Leaving Social Media*. Find her online at ameliahruby.com and offthegrid.fun. (Please invite her on your podcast, she'd love to be a guest!)